I0822599

DATELINE: WORLD

20 Dispatches from the Earth & One from Hell

Brick Tower Press
Habent Sua Fata Libelli

Brick Tower Press
Manhanset House
Shelter Island Hts., New York 11965-0342
Tel: 212-427-7139
bricktower@aol.com • www.BrickTowerPress.com

Library of Congress Cataloging-in-Publication Data
Nieuwsma, Milton J.
Dateline: World—20 Dispatches from the Earth & One from Hell
p. cm.
Includes bibliographical references

1. Language Arts & Disciplines / Journalism.
2. Literary Collections / Essays.
3. Biography & Autobiography / Editors, Jouranlists, Publishers. I. Title.

September 2023

ISBN: 978-1-876969-09-7, Hardcover
ISBN: 978-1-899694-17-7, Trade Paper

DATELINE: WORLD

20 Dispatches from the Earth
& One from Hell

Milton J.
Nieuwsma

Foreword by Tom Stites
Two-Time Pulitzer Prize Winner

ALSO BY MILTON NIEUWSMA

Kinderlager
(2000 "Best Book for Teens")

Surviving Auschwitz
(basis for the Emmy-winning PBS special)

They Will Be Victors
(with Robert Wollack)

Earth Angels
(with Peter VandenBosch)

Inventing America
(companion to the acclaimed PBS series)

Miracle on Chestnut Street

To my friends and colleagues, past and present,
in the vanishing world of print journalism

"All the world's a stage,
And all the men and women merely Players;
They have their exits and their entrances.
And one man in his time plays many parts."

William Shakespeare, *As You Like It*

Contents

Foreword

A favorite shelf in my bookcase leads with *By-Line: Ernest Hemingway,* a compendium of journalism the great novelist wrote from Europe and Africa to support himself as he worked on his fiction. Right next to it is *Ernie's War,* dispatches by Ernie Pyle, the most famous of World War II correspondents. Nestling with these are books of superb but less-famous journalists, all friends and great writers for newspapers in Chicago, St. Louis, Philadelphia and Kansas City. Milton Nieuwsma's fine volume, the one you're holding now, joins this shelf of honor.

In this era when so much of our news coverage comes at us in ceaseless blizzards of tiny digital chunks, much of it of dubious accuracy, it's easy to forget that people once loved slow-moving newspapers. Once a day the papers delivered, all in one package, not only the day's news, sports scores, comic strips, and advice columnists, but also informal literature that brought readers pleasure while often widening their minds. This icing for the newspaper cake came to us from journalists, both local and distant, who were superb storytellers.

Milt is a master of this craft. He takes us to the Arctic, the Antarctic, the Amazon and the Nile. He also takes us to the Field of Dreams in Dyersville, Iowa, where the great baseball movie was filmed. And through a fine profile, he takes us into the mind of the mighty novelist James Mitchener. Milt holds him in some awe, and his piece makes it clear why.

The gruesome torture and killing of 14-year-old Emmett Till was a crucial spur to the civil rights movement, and in my decades as a journalist I thought I'd read enough about this heart-wrenching event to be confident that I knew all I needed to know. But no. Milt's research for his retrospective account opened my mind to much meaningful and troubling new detail about the death of the Black youth from Chicago who went to Mississippi to visit family in 1955. I'm shaking my head in sadness as I write this paragraph. There is information here that everybody needs to know.

Reporters like Milt who traveled to far-away places came to be called correspondents. Why? Perhaps you had an aunt who wrote letters so interesting that the family pounced on them as soon as they hit the mailbox. The aunt was one kind of great correspondent. Newspaper correspondents whose prose became familiar in your household could inspire a similar response.

Milt Nieuwsma exemplifies this all-but-lost craft. But his work is in no way lost and its value still leaps out of the page at the reader. The book you're holding offers 21 examples that appeared in major newspapers including *The Los Angeles Times* and *Chicago Tribune;* in his hometown *Holland Sentinel* in Michigan, and in countless other papers through syndication—profiles of fascinating people, insightful commentary pieces, and finely crafted letters from every continent.

In this era where almost every TV news screen screams BREAKING NEWS, let's pause to note that news can be slow and deep—and a pleasure to relax and read. If only we all had aunts who write so well.

Tom Stites
Newburyport, Mass.

Tom Stites, as a ranking editor for major newspapers including *The New York Times, Chicago Tribune* and *Kansas City Star,* supervised reporting projects that have won an array of major journalism awards, including two Pulitzer Prizes. His writings on journalism and democracy have been widely published.

Author's Note

This book is for people with short attention spans like mine. Except for an occasional foray into how we humans treat the planet and each other, each piece stands alone. Read one at bedtime each night; it won't take you but fifteen minutes. Not only that, when you turn off the light, you'll know a little more about the world than you did before.

MJN

Part One: Places

A student with an Israeli flag walks along the tracks at Auschwitz-Birkenau where 1.5 million people, mainly Jews, were transported to their deaths.

Auschwitz, Poland

The Remembrance

JUST OUTSIDE THE VILLAGE of Oswiecim in southern Poland, a faint sun shines through the poplars that surround the killing chambers at Auschwitz-Birkenau. At the end of the track a few hundred well-bundled souls, many walking with canes, gather around a monument to pray for the dead and grapple with the wounds of their past.

The resonant voice of cantor Moshe Stern pierces the chilly silence as he sings El Moleh Rahamin, "Oh merciful God."

Elie Wiesel, an Auschwitz survivor and Nobel Peace Prize laureate, steps to the microphone and declares: "Please, God, do not have mercy on those who created this place. God of forgiveness, do not forgive those murderers of Jewish children here."

The date is January 26, 1995, the day before the 50th anniversary of the camp's liberation. The occasion: a ceremony attended mostly by Jews in protest to the Polish government's planned ceremony for the next day. Their objection: that the official ceremony does not include the *kaddish*, the Jewish prayer for the dead, or acknowledge that most of the camp's victims were Jews.

A few non-Jews like Sigmond Sobolewski, a Polish Catholic, join the protest. One of the first inmates of Auschwitz, he wears number 88 on his faded prison stripes and a sandwich board that proclaims: "We the Christians are also guilty of the Holocaust."

The next day thousands more—Jews and non-Jews—gather to mark the official anniversary of the camp's liberation. Elie Wiesel, flanked by Polish President Lech Walesa, walks through the gate that contains the inscription, *Arbeit Macht Frei* ("Work Makes You Free").

Again, there are speeches. "Close your eyes, my friends, and listen," Wiesel exhorts the crowd. "Listen to the silent screams of terrified mothers. Listen to the prayers of anguished old men and women. Listen to the tears of children."

President Walesa follows him to the microphone, a tremor in his voice as he speaks: "This is a bleak road for all nations, but mostly for the Jewish people." The words *but mostly for the Jewish people* are penned into his manuscript. Neither speaker mentions their meeting the night before in which Wiesel persuaded the Polish president to point out that Jews were the main target at Auschwitz.

A third of the way around the world, in Cambridge, Mass., Frieda Tenenbaum and her childhood friends Tova Friedman and Rachel Hyams quietly observe their 50th "birthday." Among the youngest of Adolf Hitler's survivors (Frieda was 10, Tova and Rachel were 6 and 7 when they were liberated from Auschwitz), they recall the Soviet troops filing through the gate on the afternoon of January 27, 1945, saving them from certain death.

It's their first reunion in 10 years. At 6 o'clock they flip on the television and watch as elite Polish guards lay wreathes on the monument. The meaning of what they see doesn't readily suggest itself; they wonder if the world will ever understand what this place was about.

I HAD MADE MY OWN pilgrimage to Auschwitz the year before. The sky was a steely gray and a brisk wind slapped my face when I entered the camp through the guardhouse. I wanted to see for myself what this place was about. I followed the path next to the railroad line that once brought prisoners into the camp. Ahead of me marched a group of seven or eight young adults, one holding an Israeli flag.

I passed the spot where Dr. Joseph Mengele—the "Angel of Death"—had selected the new arrivals as they were herded out of the cattle cars: a motion to the left meant the gas chambers; to the right meant slave labor. Then I passed the women's camp on my left and on my right the *Kinderlager*, the children's camp. All that remained of the barracks were rows of spindly brick chimneys, mute testimony to the horrors of this place, ersatz tombstones in a vast and nameless graveyard.

Eventually, I made my way to the far end of the camp. At the end of the tracks stood a monument flanked by broken slabs of concrete—the remains of Crematoria II and III—left just as they were when the retreating Nazis blew them up. I walked over to the monument where marble plaques in nineteen languages lined the base. I found one in English that read:

Forever let this place be
a cry of despair
and a warning to humanity
where the Nazis murdered
about one and a half
million
men, women and children,
mainly Jews
from various countries
of Europe.
Auschwitz-Birkenau
1940-1945

After finding some wild flowers to place on the monument, I followed a short path to the remains of Crematorium II and descended the stairs into the undressing room. Numbness closed in on me like a fist when I imagined Tova and Rachel standing under the fake shower heads wrapped in their towels. I imagined the SS guard at the iron door flipping furiously through the papers on his clipboard looking for their numbers. I could hear his shouts: "*Darouse!*" (Get them out!) "Wrong block!"

Next to where the storehouses once stood—what the prisoners dubbed "Canada" because they imagined Canada to be a country of great wealth—a marble plaque at the ruins of Crematorium IV caught my eye. It told how the ovens were blown up by the *Sonderkommando*, Jewish prisoners who had been forced to empty the gas chambers and feed the corpses into the fire. I thought of Roza Robota and her fellow prisoners who had smuggled in dynamite and Roza's last words, in Hebrew: "Be strong, have courage!" as an SS guard lowered a rope around her neck. The plaque noted the date of the revolt: October 7, 1944.

I looked at the digital calendar on my watch: OCT 7. It was 50 years ago to the day that Frieda and her mother descended the stairs where I now stood and heard the explosion that sent them back to their barracks.

In my mind's eye I see hundreds of women and children being led to the gas chambers. I hear them crying. I hear their prayers. I see the iron gate that says WORK MAKES YOU FREE and hear the musicians play as new prisoners are brought in. I see a pile of human hair—young girls' braids and women's bouffants—brown, blond, black, and red. I see a washroom covered in blood from young men who put up a fight on their way to being executed. I see a room full of suitcases scrawled with family names and wonder if *Grossman* or *Tenenbaum* or *Greenspan* might be among them.

I see Rudolf Hoess, the camp's commandant, holding back his emotions while his SS underlings rip children from their screaming mothers. Oddly, I think of William Styron's portrayal of him in *Sophie's Choice* as an affectionate father and family man forced into bestial conduct out of fear of not following his superiors' orders.

SIGMUND SOBOLEWSKI, prisoner 88, watches as the elite Polish guards place their wreathes on the monument. He's wearing the same sandwich board as the day before with the words *We the Christians are also guilty of the Holocaust.* As a Christian myself, I feel the shame.

The people gathered at the monument know *what* happened at Auschwitz. But who can tell *why*? In my own search I find only omens, not answers, a few forgotten relics from history's trash heap: a silver plate, engraved in 1160 and discovered at a German convent, depicting Jews marching into an oven (the Latin inscription around the rim reads: "Because she rejects Christ, the synagogue deserves hell"); a sermon Martin Luther preached in 1543 instructing his listeners how Jews, the Christ-killers, should be treated ("First, their synagogues shall be set on fire, and whatever does not burn shall be covered with dirt"); an account of the three-hundredth anniversary of the Passion Play at Oberammergau in 1934, which became a showcase for the Nazis' anti-Semitic campaign (of the play's ten major actors, nine were Nazis; the lone exception was the actor playing Judas).

A half-century after the war, I see the Star of David and the word *Jude* scrawled on a storefront in Tomaszow Mazowiecki, the girls' home town in central Poland. I ask the owner of a restaurant off the town square if there are any Jews left in Tomaszow, and he dismisses the notion with a wave of his hand.

Why Auschwitz?

We look for answers, but they are fragmentary and incomplete; they don't satisfy and probably never will. My friends Tova and Frieda and Rachel were among the handful of children who survived Hitler's most notorious death camp. They can't tell why Auschwitz happened either.

Yet they do tell us *what* happened, and perhaps that's enough. Because it's the living who speak for the dead; through them we hear the silent screams of terrified mothers and hear the tears of children. To turn away is to kill them a second time. But to listen is to confront the monster that lurks in the human soul.

This story was first published in the *Chicago Tribune*, April 18, 1998.

Yakutat, Alaska

The Ice Menace Cometh

AS THE PLANE APPROACHED the tiny fishing village of Yakutat on Alaska's southeastern panhandle, I looked out the window for signs of Kah Lituya, the legendary monster guarding Disenchantment Bay. Here it is said when strangers intrude, he throws up giant waves to drive them away.

Since I was no stranger here, I didn't expect to find him. But at the north end of Disenchantment Bay, ringed by spectacular snow-capped peaks, I caught a glimpse of another monster – this one far more menacing than Kah Lituya.

Some 300 feet high and five miles wide, it was sliding down a crevasse in the St. Elias Mountains, pushing a massive pile of rocks and gravel in front of it. This monster had a name too: Hubbard Glacier.

Geologists were calling it a world-class natural event. The Hubbard had woken from a centuries-long deep sleep to begin its ominous advance, surging ahead by as much as 40 feet a day. It had sealed off a fjord, trapping porpoises and harbor seals, and now it threatened disaster to Yakutat's 450-odd residents – most of them Tlingit Indians (pronounced Klin-Kits) who have fished the waters here for 600 years.

During the summer of 1962 I made my first trip to Yakutat as a 20-year-old college student in search of a fortune. Red and silver salmon, I'd heard, were bringing $1.25 apiece

Me in 1986 displaying a sea lion's tooth, a gift my Tlingit friends gave me signifying my status as an an honorary tribal member.

at the local cannery, and you could net 300 or more in a single catch.

Like most get-rich-quick schemes, this one didn't pan out. After three months I returned home with $20 in my pocket and a summer's worth of memories. But my most prized possession was a four-inch sea lion's tooth my indigenous friends gave me before I left, conferring on me the title "honorary Tlingit."

So when I heard about the glacier, I had to go back; one does not ignore one's friends in a time of crisis, and I still had some there.

One of them was William ("Ish") Thomas, a tribal elder and fountain of Tlingit lore who once told me about the Raven who turned himself into a shaman so he could "help people and set things right."

There were others—people like Fred Henry and Susie Abraham—all of them engaged now in an immense struggle against nature in which time and human ingenuity would determine the outcome.

Then there was Caroline Mallott, my heartthrob from the summer of '62. She was 18 then, and her Tlingit mother and Caucasian father ran the general store on Yakutat's main street, a mud-clogged thoroughfare that snaked along the bank of Monti Bay.

It didn't matter that she was married now to Larry Powell, the village mayor, and had three grown kids. A generation had passed since I'd even thought of her. Now she was being quoted in *Time* magazine about her people being the subject of some scientist's experiment. "If they feel sympathy," she said, "it's for the porpoises and seals. What about us?"

Thus, with my own resolve to set things right, I took off once again for Yakutat to see my Tlingit friends, my travel bag in hand and the sea lion's tooth in my pocket, proving—just in case I needed it—that I was still one of them.

What I encountered when I stepped off the plane 10 hours later was a horde of TV crews and fish and wildlife people describing their latest—and futile—attempts to airlift the porpoises and seals out of nearby Russell Fjord.

Now a glacial lake, the fjord's dammed-up seawater was changing to freshwater from the mountain runoff, driving the sea mammals' food supply (mostly fish and crabs) under the freshwater surface and depleting the oxygen from the salt water.

I wormed my way through the terminal to the Yakutat Lodge 100 yards away. Inside, I met Fred Henry, now 42, who was sitting at the manager's desk looking irritated. When I introduced myself, he regarded me suspiciously at first, but when I produced the sea lion's tooth he greeted me like an old friend.

We started with small talk about my summer in Yakutat. Did we or did we not meet the summer of '62? Neither of us could remember. The subject shifted to what was irritating him.

"This media circus is ridiculous," he said. "There's been so much money spent on a few animals—save the seals, save the porpoises. No one would pay this much attention to a cow drowning in the Mississippi delta or a pig that's dying in a snow storm in Colorado. It's an impossible task to start with. The seals are a food source to us, and there are all kinds of these animals throughout the bay. It's not like they're endangered."

Henry, the son of a Tlingit Indian chief, was more worried that the lake would spill over its southern banks and wash out the Situk River, the artery that carries the blood of Tlingit life in Yakutat.

"More attention ought to be given to the plight of this town," he said. "We're going to be economically hard hit, and no one seems to be able to make a decision about whether or not to build a channel for this river or to try and blow out the glacier and save this town.

"Yakutat could be dying right now because of this river. This is a preventable disaster, and no one is making any effort to channel this river or stop the washout of the Situk."

Pips Petersen, who met me for breakfast the next morning, looked little like the hard-drinking, care-be-damned teenager I knew in 1962. Now 43, he was thoroughly domesticated with a lovely wife and two young daughters and headed the local native corporation, a Tlingit-run business conglomerate formed after the Alaska Native Claims Settlement Act of 1971.

As we drove through town in his pickup truck, I saw other changes too. Gone were the mud-clogged roads, replaced by asphalt pavement. A new highway had been built above the road that still ran past Mallott's General Store and the local cannery. The old two-room school was now a courthouse. Some of the shanties were still around, but here and there a satellite dish popped out between the corrugated rooftops.

We wheeled into the turnoff at the local senior citizens home (also built since 1962) where Pips took me in to see William Thomas. Now 75, "Ish", as we fondly called him (meaning "father" in Tlingit), was one of five tribal chiefs in the village, head of the Eagle clan.

"The glacier is just like a human being," he said in his broken Tlingit dialect. "That's why you talk to it, so you don't fall off too much while you're hunting seal. If you laugh by it, it gets mean-like, and it will chase you. If you make it mad, it growls like a bear. Right now it's mad, and I don't know why."

Next door, Susie Abraham, 85, talked about her own childhood teachings "not to tamper with nature."

"The old ways, the old customs, are being lost," she lamented, as she slipped a cup of tea into a microwave oven. "This place where we live," she said, "belongs to the great glacier. We are put here for a little while to enjoy God's creation, then we go. But the great glacier stays."

Not everyone shared her fatalism. Back at the Yakutat Lodge, Pete Kline, 51, plunked a $50 bill down on the bar, ordered a Canadian Club and soda for himself and drinks for everyone in the house.

"This glacier is much ado about nothing," he snorted. "The Situk River has about as much chance of overflowing as the Russians have of bombing Alaska. If it happens, it'll be seven months before I die of old age."

The next day I finally got to see my old summer flame, Caroline Mallott, who now lives above the store her mother and father ran the summer of '62. "That summer is a haze to me," she said, not doing much for my ego. It was also the summer her husband-and-mayor-to-be, Larry Powell, now 46, came to Yakutat on a fishing boat, got a job in the cannery, and stayed. I asked him if he had ever read *The Mayor of Casterbridge,* the Thomas Hardy novel. He hadn't.

Earlier that week, Larry had met with an aide to Alaska Senator Ted Stevens to discuss a proposal for funding a channel to drain the water from the lake. He was hoping to get the U.S. Army Corps of Engineers to do it but didn't seem all that optimistic.

"Chances are it would take two years to complete the cost-benefit-ratio analysis," he said.

Meanwhile, the livelihood of two-thirds of Yakutat's work force would be wiped out, he said. The flood waters would contaminate Yakutat's wells with salt water and lap onto the runway of the local airport, cutting off Yakutat's only transportation link to the outside world.

"A new ice age is taking over here," added Caroline. "If the Situk floods over, there would be just absolute poverty in this town."

From the kitchen table Caroline and I looked out over the bay that geologists said could turn into a massive ice sheet again, just as it did 800 years ago. Larry was on the telephone.

"That was the U.S. Geological Survey," he said after he hung up. "They're saying the ice dam could break through within 24 hours. That will buy us time (to build the channel), but not much. Once that glacier moves, it just keeps moving."

Ten days later, the ice dam finally did break through, but scientists predicted the surging Hubbard would only block up Russell Fjord again, and this time it would be for good as the glacier continued to build up its mass. But for now, nature had granted a reprieve.

Fred Henry met me back at the Yakutat Lodge. It had been two months since he had a day off, but he promised to take me on a little trip.

We rode in his ancient skiff up the Situk River along the banks filled with undergrowth. Half a mile up the river he nosed the skiff into the bank, and we fought our way through the brush.

After several hundred feet we found ourselves in a silent strand of tall Sitka spruce. Under the trees stood a concrete tomb, the name "Jim" outlined in stones on the top.

"Situk Jim was my great granduncle," Fred said. "My Indian name is Situk Jim. I inherited that name." He pointed to the other graves nearby.

"That's my grandfather, Samson Harry, over there, and my great grandfather, Situk Harry. Situk Jim and Situk Harry were brothers, and they used to own this river.

"This river is where I was born, and this is where I want to be buried. But if this river washes away, all this will be lost."

A profound sadness came over me as we left. The washout of the Situk would not only affect the living but wipe out the graves of Fred's ancestors as well. Was this the great glacier's idea of a practical joke? Was it laughing back?

The scientists were saying the fishing grounds would be good for at least another year. But what did they know? By then the reporters and conservationists would be gone, and Yakutat—my Tlingit home—would be forgotten.

This story was first published in the *Chicago Tribune*, November 6, 1986.

Bora, Peru

A Vanishing Eden

IN THE THATCHED-ROOF village of Bora, deep in the jungle of the Peruvian Amazon, a wooden drum signaled the arrival of the *M.V. Rio Amazonas*. Two naked boys scurried down the riverbank and grabbed a line tossed out to them.

As we climbed ashore, dozens of other youngsters charged down the bank like a regiment of ants, shouting "Gringos! Gringos!" All the while their eyes were fixed on our plastic bags filled with crewing gum, suckers, balloons, mirrors, combs, ballpoint pens and other trinkets.

Our guide, Beder Chavez, led us into a large thatched hut that served as a community center. He motioned our little group—15 Americans and one New Zealander—to sit down on a log.

The village, Beder explained, was populated by two Indian tribes—the Bora and the Huitoto. For thousands of years, they enthusiastically feasted on one another (cannibalism in the region took place as recently as the mid-1900s). Since then, Beder assured us, the encroachment of civilization has forced them to make "other eating arrangements."

More than anyone, Beder could appreciate the change. Born in the jungle 35 years ago, he left his native village at age 14, went to school in Iquitos about 150 miles upriver,

A member of the Amazon's Yagua tribe wears a garment made of shredded palm fiber.

taught himself English, and set about writing a book about growing up in the Amazon rain forest.

After he spoke, the villagers broke into a lively anaconda dance. At their urging, several of us joined in to the rhythmic beating of a pair of manguare (hollowed-out hardwood logs) and the chanting of Bora men and women dressed in painted bark skin. Near the door stood a barefoot mother nursing her child.

When the dancing was over, the trading began. The baskets, beads and blowguns were beautiful and strange. Negotiating was a family affair, involving consultation mostly between mothers and children in a language we didn't know. Their disarming smiles belied their once-peculiar dining habits and reduced our bargaining skills to zero.

A few yards from where my wife was trading a mirror for a necklace of paiche scales, one of the dancers, an extraordinarily beautiful young woman with black paint streaked across her cheeks, dropped her bark-skin dress unabashedly to her waist and pulled on an Adidas T-shirt.

With every plastic comb and stick of chewing gum we left behind, weren't we unwitting accomplices to the corruption of their ancient way of life?

"We're witnessing the last few years of the Amazon in its present state," Beder said later. "Farther south, in Brazil, it's much worse." He told about how the rain forests there are disappearing at the rate of 5,000 acres a day because of the exploitation of oil and minerals, and how much of it is the fault of Brazil's government, which has failed to hold unscrupulous landowners in check.

"Four million Indians once lived in the Amazon basin," he said. "Now only about 120,000 remain. Even the birds and animals have to go deeper inside to get away."

Beder then explained why he was leading us through this 350-mile stretch of the upper Amazon that runs from Iquitos, Peru, to Leticia, Colombia, acting as intermediary between our little group from the 20th century and the primordial world of the jungle. "I'm trying to alert the rest of the world to the need to preserve this river," he said. "Perhaps it will be worth more as a tourist site than as an industrial wasteland."

For the five of us who flew down from Miami, this was our first jaunt into the South American jungle. After a night's layover at the Crillon Hotel in Lima, we flew over the Andes to Iquitos, a bustling river-front town (population 200,000) where the north-flowing Ucayali River turns into the Amazon.

The streets were lined with motorcycle-powered rickshaws. We hired one to take us to neighboring Belen, a floating village where the houses are built on stilts and pontoons. Here the river rises as much as 35 feet during the rainy season, but now it was low. Garbage and dead fish littered the streets. In the marketplace fly-infested meat and vegetables lay rotting in the sun. The squalor was punctuated by the sight of a man carrying a huge bunch of green bananas on his back.

Here we caught our first sight of the mighty Amazon. Originating high in the Andes 1,700 miles to the south, its name changes four times before it turns east at Iquitos and flows another 2,300 miles into the Atlantic. The river is second only to the Nile in length but is the largest in volume, draining 200 major tributaries into an area three-quarters the size of the United States. Its flow is 11 times greater than the Mississippi's. Its vegetation represents almost half of the remaining forest on earth and supplies half of the world's new oxygen. During flood season it discharges three trillion gallons of water a day into the Atlantic, enough to supply New York City with water for nine years.

We also learned how the Amazon got its name. When the Spanish explorer, Francisco de Orellano, first ventured onto it in 1542, he reported encountering battling warrior women, each of whom "made as much war as 10 men." The fearsome females were dubbed "Amazons," after a Greek myth. Like Mark Twain's Mississippi, this river is the stuff of tall tales.

That night we set out from Iquitos on board the *M.V. Rio Amazonas*, one of a fleet of Amazon riverboats owned by Paul

Wright, 54, a U.S. ex-patriot and business entrepreneur. He greeted us amiably in the ship's dining room wearing a blue Los Angeles Dodgers baseball cap and a green "Amazon Camp" T-shirt. He described how he had been a tour operator in Los Angeles, got tired of the pressure, and fled to Iquitos 20 years ago to start his jungle camp. His wife didn't share his enthusiasm. "She went back to California with her blow-dryer," he said.

Wright showed us his ship, a diesel-powered triple-decker resurrected five years before from the abandoned hull of an 1896 Scottish cargo ship. "I designed it on the back of a paper bag," he said. The 146-foot vessel boasts 16 air-conditioned cabins (each with a private shower and toilet) and an 18-member crew that includes a witch doctor who was once a medic in the Peruvian army. Four times a month it makes the run from Iquitos to Leticia. Passengers are mostly Americans, Australians and New Zealanders, and thus English-speaking.

On the middle deck we discovered an open-air bar that stilled our apprehension as we set out into the black moonless night. The bar prices were cause for rejoicing: 60 cents for beer, 25 cents for Cokes, 75 cents for pisco sours—a frothy, sweet but deceptive punch.

Early the next morning I stood on the foredeck sipping coffee as I watched the sun rise over this uninhabited land. I felt serenely blessed as the jungle drifted silently by, not a soul in sight. The stillness was broken by two squawking macaws in ferocious pursuit of one another.

Up in the pilot's cabin I spoke with the captain, Cesar Vasquez, who had been cruising the Amazon for so many years it seemed like he was married to it. "This river, she's like a woman," he said. "You can't see beneath her skin, but you know her mood by what you feel. She has her rules, and you must play by them."

Finally I spotted human habitation—three or four stilt houses spewing plumes of smoke from breakfast fires. These were the homes of the *mestizos riberenos* (river dwellers), who slashed and burned patches of forest along the riverbank and farmed the soil until it petered out. Then they would move on to another spot along the river and repeat the process. Theirs was an unmechanized, non-monetary, self-sufficient world.

Even in daytime there was little traffic on the river. Tiny children, barely old enough to walk, frantically pursued our ship in a hand-hewn dugout until it turned over in the water. Once we encountered a *collectivo*, a grungy-looking ferry boat with wooden kegs strapped to the top, a loose chicken or two on the deck, and people sleeping in hammocks or leaning glumly over the rails.

Each day on our river cruise we stopped at a village. At Bora, where we watched the anaconda dancers, I learned something of the terrible history of the Huitoto people—how they were abused and slaughtered by European rubber traders at the turn of the century. Only a decade ago the Peruvian government moved them to the river to live near their deadly enemies, the Bora. The Bora are less acculturated than the Huitoto and still use hallucinogens in their tribal rituals. Even so, the Huitoto still shun contact with the outside world.

For the most part, though, the tribal merger has been peaceful. The children (for whom the government now decrees compulsory education for five years) even share a one-room schoolhouse.

Near another village we visited the riverbank farm of a *mestizo*. The 81-year-old owner was harvesting sugarcane when we arrived. He laid down his machete to greet us and led us into his house, where his wife was squeezing pulp from a cassava root into a bucket. She then mixed it with fermented spit to make a liquor called *masato*. As she was about to offer us some, we made a polite but hasty retreat.

Not until we reached Pevas, a Jesuit missionary village near the mouth of the Ampiyacu River, did we encounter signs of the white man's world. A stucco steeple with a cross on top presided over a cluster of thatched huts. An Evinrudepowered skiff zoomed out from the riverbank, ostensibly in search of converts.

Late in the afternoon we made our first foray into the jungle's hot interior. A thick canopy of foliage filtered out the sunlight. Spider webs and termite nests the size of footballs clung to the infinite-seeming vegetation. Ropelike vines, straight out of Tarzan movie, hung 40 feet from the tops of trees. Massive roots of the mora tree reached out in all directions, impeding our progress. Ants and chiggers crawled beneath our feet. A few hours later our little group emerged, sweat-drenched but otherwise unharmed.

After dinner, fortified by pisco sours, we set out in a motor launch to look for caimans (Amazon crocodiles) on the Cochaquinas River. With the motor off we drifted quietly in the pitch dark listening to the whoops and chatters that emanated from the jungle. Then in the beam of Beder's flashlight we spotted the beady red eyes of a caiman. Beder crept cautiously out of the launch and reached down to grab it by the tail. It slithered away. Later, as we headed back to our ship, the radiant sheen of the Milky Way reflected over the water. We were four degrees below the equator, and the stars seemed close enough to touch.

The next morning we went piranha fishing along the banks of the Atacuari River. I had heard about how piranhas, at the smell of blood, could rip a man to shreds in minutes. But down here, Beder assured us, "Piranhas don't eat people; people eat piranhas." The fish are actually quite small with silver skins, flaming orange bellies, and tiny razor-sharp teeth. We baited our hooks with red meat. I managed one or two nibbles until a particularly vicious one snapped my line.

At lunch the cook claimed he fed piranhas to us in his fish stew, but nobody believed him. The night before, he tried to tell us we were eating monkey meat, which turned out to be chicken cacciatore. Despite his good-natured attempts to deceive us, the food he served was delicious. Lunch and dinner consisted of broiled paiche and catfish with yellow boiled potatoes and fresh hearts of palm washed down with mango juice.

I was glad to know the pink dolphins had been spared his skillet. Once we watched a whole school heave themselves out of the water like children at play. "The Indians don't kill them because they're afraid it will bring bad luck," Beder said, adding that if an Indian girl gets pregnant before she's married, "it's the pink dolphin that did it."

Another river excursion took us to a lagoon covered with giant Victoria Regia water lilies. Their pads, we were told, grow up to six feet in diameter—strong enough to support a child. On an overhanging branch a kingfisher with dark blue wings gazed down at us as we stepped on them to test the claim. Most of our party left with dry feet.

We ended our cruise at the riverfront town of Leticia, where the borders of Peru, Colombia and Brazil come together. Known for its populace of smugglers and outlaws, Leticia has all the charm of a spaghetti western. Hard tattooed men and rosy-cheeked women glared at us from verandas and saloon doors as we made our way from the harbor to the airport in a battered VW van.

A few hours later we were back in Iquitos, where we spent the last night of our jungle adventure at Paul Wright's Amazon Camp. Surrounded by jungle, all the buildings were thatched and on stilts and connected by a long kerosine-lit walkway. Each room had its own bathroom and kerosine lamp. In the camp's thatched-roof bar, two bilingual parrots whose vocabularies consisted mostly of "hello" and "*vamos!*" kept up a running commentary on the patrons until a wooden drum called us to dinner.

On our last day we ventured out from the jungle camp to a nearby village where we met a Yagua Indian dressed in a skirt and headdress of shredded palm fiber, his face painted a fierce red. He had a beautiful old blowgun that he demonstrated. This amazing hardwood device was so weighted that he could easily hold the seven-foot length in front of his chin.

He handed the blowgun to me, along with a toothpick-thin dart wrapped in a kapok wad. I imagined myself as Tommy Markham, the hero of John Boorman's film "The Emerald Forest," who was kidnapped by Indians and raised in the Amazon jungle. He could handle a blowgun as well as anybody. I inserted the dart, aimed the blowgun at a tree, and missed.

It then struck me that it may have been this man's ancestors Francisco de Orellano encountered when he sailed onto this river over 450 years ago. Was it their skirts and headdresses that made him think they were the warrior women of Amazon lore? Had I at last met primordial man?

Just as I was complimenting myself on this insight, my new-found friend with his painted face and ancient blowgun lit a cigarette. Deep in the Amazon jungle, "civilization" had found him too.

This story was first published in the *Los Angeles Times*, May 22, 1988.

Aswan, Egypt

Time Travel on the Nile

AS THE *M.S. NILE SOVEREIGN* got ready to tie up in the locks near Aswan, Captain Tolba fired an Arabic curse at a bungling deckhand, "May your house burn down!"

It was already past midnight. I gazed out from the foredeck into the pitch-black night, a total stranger in a faraway land. I turned to look at Tolba in the pilot's cabin. Bronze-skinned, wrinkle-faced and garbed in a turban, sandals and galabia (a robe-like garment), he appeared old enough to have been at the helm of Cleopatra's barge.

The fate of 26 passengers was in his hands. Yet I felt oddly reassured by this old man whose language and customs we didn't know. To him, the Nile was home. For the rest of us, this was a journey into another world, altogether ancient and mysterious. From our floating time machine, we witnessed 5,000 years of civilization come and go.

It was along this ancient river that civilization took seed and grew, where tools of human intelligence like mathematics, physics and astronomy were invented, giving man the capacity to build great pyramids and navigate the earth's waters and—nearly five millennia later—to create computers and explore the planets.

Garbed in a turban and galabia, this Nubian desert dweller seeks protection from the wind and sand.

But it's also where human engineering and ingenuity, in more recent times, have sucked the spirit out of thousands of its more unfortunate inhabitants.

The world's longest river, the Nile begins as a tiny trickle of water deep in the heart of Africa. Some 2,285 miles later, this stream of water (called the White Nile) merges at Khartoum, Sudan, with its sister, the 1,080-mile-long Blue Nile, and together they continue the journey 1,900 miles north to the Mediterranean through one of the fiercest deserts in the world.

"This is the greatest place on earth," proclaimed our guide, Bassam el Shamma, a 28-year-old archaeology graduate of the University of Cairo, as he greeted us at Abu Simbel, the first stop on our Nile time-trip just north of the Sudan border. A cluster of mud huts broke the vast expanse of uninhabitable desert. The air was so dry that dust congealed in our throats. Nearby stood two gleaming Air Egypt DC-9s, waiting like giant vultures to scoop up any children who might come out to inspect.

It soon became apparent what attracted Bassam to this place. He led us to an artificial hill in which four gigantic colossi of Ramses II, the most powerful and prolific of Egypt's ancient pharaohs (he's said to have married 50 wives and fathered 150 children) gazed out across Lake Nasser. Bassam's eyes twinkled. "You know about Egypt's overpopulation problem. It began with Ramses more than 3,300 years ago."

Bassam explained how Ramses' temple was carved into a cliff overlooking the Nile. Beside his temple stood that of his queen, Nefertari. Built about 1270 B.C., these magnificent structures occupied the southern reaches of Ramses' empire. Engulfed by invading sands over the centuries, the temples lay hidden until they were discovered by a Swiss traveler named Johann Burckhardt in 1813.

A century-and-half later, it was UNESCO to the rescue. When the Nile's water began rising behind the newly constructed Aswan Dam, UNESCO (the United Nations Educational, Scientific and Cultural Organization) spent four years and $40 million to dig the temples out of the sand, cut them into huge blocks, and raise them to the hill overlooking the reservoir. Say what you will about the $40 million, Ramses' resurrection is a monument to man's ingenuity.

A few hours later, we boarded a plane for a short hop to Aswan, where Gamal Abdul Nasser, with Russian help, built the greatest public work to be undertaken in Egypt since the pyramids. Completed in 1964, Aswan's High Dam is some 350 feet high and two-and-a-half miles long. Its reservoir, Lake Nasser, is one of the largest man-made lakes in the world, stretching 300 miles south through virtually uninhabited desert into Sudan. Nasser believed the dam was needed to increase food production for Egypt's soaring population.

I thought of Joseph, the slave of Old Testament times, who interpreted Pharoah's dream of seven years of plenty followed by seven years of famine. Thanks to the Aswan Dam, the cycle of floods and droughts that once plagued Egypt occurs no longer, but the dam has created problems of its own.

Now it blocks the fertile silt that once washed down from central Africa. Unreplenished, key agricultural lands in the Nile delta are threatened by erosion. Add to that the displacement of 100,000 Nubians whose ancient homeland behind the dam is now a drowned museum. Observed Bassam sadly, "Sometimes human solutions fall short."

Yet the city of Aswan is probably the most picturesque of any along the Nile. High above the water, from the terrace of the Old Cataract Hotel (immortalized by Agatha Christie in her best-seller, *Death on the Nile*), we watched small sailing boats called feluccas glide by, while on the horizon stood the domed silhouette of the Aga Khan mausoleum.

We slipped into a felucca and sailed to Elephantine Island, where a massive "nilometer" carved by the ancient Romans into an elephant-shaped boulder once recorded the annual flood level of the Nile.

At Aswan we boarded the *Sovereign*, the newest cruiser to join the Nile's growing fleet. My wife and I were the only Americans on board.

"Only about five percent of our passengers are American," said Dennis Cook, our British-born cruise director and a veteran of many Nile trips. "Since Camp David (the summit between Israeli Prime Minister Menachem Begin and Egyptian President Anwar Sadat in 1979 that produced the Sinai peace treaty) we've had a dramatic increase in tourism here, but relatively few Americans come. Too bad, really, because Egyptians like Americans," and he added with a wry smile, "perhaps more than they like the British."

It's no wonder. In 1962 Nasser threw the British out, which enabled Egypt to regain its sovereignty after centuries of foreign domination. Now American aid pours into Egypt at the rate of $2 billion a year. When the turbaned ticket-taker at the 2,300-year-old temple of the goddess Hathor asked me if I was English and I said, "No, I'm American," he shook my hand so vigorously I thought he wanted it as a souvenir.

At Kom Ombo, 25 miles north of Aswan, the locals were less gregarious. Anyone familiar with their history could understand why. Near a Roman temple overlooking the Nile, we encountered some glum-looking Nubians who had been forced to leave their home when it vanished below Lake Nasser.

"When the lake filled up," said Bassam, "the Sudanese Nubians went south and the Egyptian Nubians came north. You can imagine the sadness when they parted, leaving parents, brothers, sisters, cousins, who lived across the border. It's something the older ones will never forget."

Late that afternoon we set sail for Luxor, watching the sun sink into the Western Desert. Looking out at the mud huts from the ship's deck, I got the impression that if time were suddenly thrust back a thousand years, life here would be unchanged. At night the only light along the shore appeared to come from bonfires. Water, rather than being pumped, is carried from the Nile in baked mud vases balanced atop the heads of black-hooded women.

In the pitch-dark desert just to the east were buried the lost remains of Nekken, where the legendary first pharaoh, Nemses, ruled Upper Egypt more than 5,000 years ago. The moonless night lent an aura of mystery to this place where some believe Egyptian civilization was born.

Our arrival at Luxor the next morning was a quantum leap back into the 20th century. Giant cruise ships lined the waterfront. Gleaming tour busses crowded the broad avenue along the river. Garishly-decorated horse carts awaited the tourists, their drivers eager to transport them to the market.

But outside the town we were back in time again, for just across the river lay the ancient Valley of the Kings, where no less than 62 pharaohs are buried in desert tombs, including Ramses II and the 19-year-old boy king Tutankhamen, whose tomb was discovered in 1922. The paintings on the walls are remarkably well-preserved and provide vivid insights into the daily lives of their former inhabitants.

Just to the south stretches the Valley of the Queens, where the sprawling 3,500-year-old temple of Queen Hatshepsut, Egypt's only female pharaoh, looks like it was carved right out of a cliff.

Luxor itself is built around the temple of Amenophis III, who reigned about 1400 B.C. More recently, in 1987 A.D., it was the site of an extravagant production of the opera "Aida."

Just to the north of Luxor lies the center of Thebes – what the ancient Greeks called "the most esteemed of places." Today it's called Karnak, and it consists of temples, chapels, giant stone pharaohs and obelisks crowned by the largest columnar structure ever built, the temple of Amun. The whole complex covers 60 acres and took 2,000 years to build as a succession of kings added their own embellishments.

In the center of Amun's temple stands a 60-foot-high colossus of Ramses II. The sight of it was absolutely intimidating. It made me wonder how Moses felt when he was brought before Pharoah to plead his case for freeing the Israelites.

I asked Bassam, "Wasn't Ramses II the one Yul Brynner played in *The Ten Commandments*?"

Bassam laughed and said, "Actually, we don't know who the pharaoh of Moses was. Some say it was Ramses II. But there's a mummy at the Egyptian museum of a pharaoh named Merenpetah, who drowned about 1200 B.C. It probably happened in the Red Sea, like what happened to the pharaoh of Moses. Have you heard the legend about the fish that ate a pharaoh's ear? If you look at that mummy it has just one ear."

Returning to Cairo after our cruise, we were jolted back into the present. Blaring horns. Stalled traffic. Diabolical drivers. Overflowing busses.

With a population of 14 million, Cairo is the largest Arab city in the world. Yet at night the whole city looks like it's illuminated by a 30-watt light bulb.

At the eastern edge of the city stands the Citadel, a 12th-century fortress just below the Muqattam hills. From here, Cairo spreads out across the Nile to the Great Pyramids, faintly visible in the Western Desert through the polluted air.

Close up, the pyramids are awesome. The three at Giza—Cheops, Chephren and Mycerinus (all named after pharaohs of the Fourth Dynasty)—rank as engineering wonders of the world. All three were built in a span of 136 years, between 2680 and 2544 B.C.

Cheops is the tallest. It stands 450 feet high and measures about 2½ football fields at its base. In the 5th century B.C., the Greek historian Herodotus wrote that it took 100,000 men more than 20 years to build the pyramid. It's no wonder. They had more than 2 million limestone blocks to haul by hand, each weighing an average of 2½ tons.

Chephren's pyramid is 10 feet shorter but still has a bit of its white casing on top. A quarter-mile causeway connects it to the Great Sphinx, which Chephren built in his own likeness to assure his immortality. It's badly eroded now, and there's much contention among archeologists over whether and how it should be restored.

No trip to Egypt would be complete without a trip to the Egyptian Museum. The museum's present building, constructed in 1902 and facing Tahrir Square in downtown Cairo, is hopelessly jammed with exhibits—more than 100,000 to be specific—with 1,700 pieces from Tutankhamen's tomb alone. Tut's treasures—the solid gold coffin, the golden throne, gold-leafed shrines, funerary beds, chariots, gilded statuettes—are displayed below huge black and white photographs taken by the English archaeologist Howard Carter when he entered the tomb in 1922. The haphazard manner in which they were strewn reminded me of my teenage son's bedroom. But then, Tut was a teenager too.

Before we left, we stopped at a humble display of seeds like those planted by Neolithic man when he first settled the Nile. Bassam, our guide, looked down at them thoughtfully and turned to our group. What followed was a 30-second outline of history that would do H.G. Wells proud.

"You see these seeds," he said. "Seeding a crop meant staying in one place. That meant waiting for the crops to grow. Waiting meant shelter. Shelter meant house. House meant furniture. Furniture meant company. Company meant wife. The wife needed protection. Protection meant weapons. Weapons meant wars. Wars meant bosses and kings. Bosses and kings meant nations.

"And that," he said, "was how the whole civilization started."

This story originally appeared in the *New York Daily News*, October 29, 1989.

Port Lockroy, Antarctica

Journey to the End of the Earth

ERNEST SHACKLETON never had it so good. Neither did his fellow Antarctic explorers who just over a century ago raced to be the first to reach the bottom of the world.

While a few like Roald Amundson made it to their destination (he was the first to reach the South Pole in 1911), others like Shackleton, best remembered for his ill-fated *Endurance* expedition in which he lost his ship but saved his crew, did not.

Still others like Robert F. Scott made it there later (he arrived just a month after Amundson) but perished in a storm, destined to spend eternity in the coldest place on earth.

The ancient Greeks dreamed of a continent at the bottom of the world, but it wasn't until 1820 that it was discovered. Antarctica's Columbus turned out to be one Fabian Gottlieb von Bellingshausen, a Baltic German officer in the Imperial Russian Navy. A year later an American sealer, John Davis, was the first to set foot on the continent.

A scattering of scientific stations followed, set up first by the British, then by a dozen or so other countries. (Three are operated by the United States—McMurdo on Ross Island, Amundsen-Scott at the South Pole, and Palmer on the Antarctic Peninsula). The first tourist ship arrived in 1966. Then came another—and then another.

Ernest Shackleton's ship, *Endurance*, fell victim to the ice in October 1915. More than a century later, in March 2022, it was found nearly intact under 10,000 feet of water.

Fast forward to the present. On any given day during the Antarctic summer (December to March), as many as 30 tourist ships may be tracked along the Antarctic Peninsula, which juts northward toward the bottom tip of South America.

What lies between is a 600-mile-wide body of water called the Drake Passage, arguably the roughest patch of ocean in the world. It's where the Atlantic and Pacific collide head-on, throwing up colossal waves that reach as high as 40 feet. Intrepid seafarers call it the Drake Shake.

For Santi Giorgi, our Argentinian guide, crossing the Drake is all in a day's work. "You have to go through hell to get to paradise," he said as we set out on the first leg of our voyage—a 100-mile cruise through the Beagle Channel from Ushuaia, Argentina, the world's southernmost city (population 80,000)—to the open sea.

How long paradise will bear up under the human invasion is another matter, not to mention the effect of global warming, a consequence of humans acting from afar.

"If things keep going at the present rate," declared Neil Horrocks, our ship's host our first day out on the Drake, "tourism in Antarctica will end in 15 years."

Since the first cruise ship arrived in 1966, a million human visitors have visited the continent. Another 100,000 are expected this year.

I thought about own our little ship, the *Hebridean Sky*, adding a puny hundred people to the invasion. How much can a hundred people affect a continent anyway—a continent twice the size of Australia, or looked at another way, as big as Mexico and the United States combined?

But every footprint makes a difference. In 1959, 12 countries including the United States created the Antarctic Treaty, declaring the continent "a natural reserve devoted to peace and science." Since then, 40 more countries have signed on, setting aside any land-grabbing notions they might have entertained.

For the most part the treaty has worked. To this day, nobody owns Antarctica but the penguins. But the explosion in tourism poses a whole new threat to its fragile eco-system: the introduction of seeds and other foreign substances like plants and insects.

To see that first-hand we first had to cross the Drake, which posed a bigger challenge than we'd bargained for. On the second day of our crossing our ship bounced around like a rubber duck, hurling my wife to the floor. It served as a warning to our fellow passengers: hold on to the handrails and don't wear socks in the bathroom. I wondered how Shackleton and his fellow mariners made it across without electronic stabilizers to keep their ships afloat, let alone GPS's to keep them on course.

After a few pain shots administered by the ship's doctor, my wife was ready to resume our joint adventure. Later that morning we passed an iceberg the size of our ship, a sign we were approaching the end of the world. I wondered how many more icebergs—and how much bigger they would get—as we drew closer.

By mid-afternoon we entered the calmer waters of the Gerlache Strait, off the northern coast of the Antarctic Peninsula. From our ship's deck we got our first close-up look at the seventh continent: gigantic, white-capped mountains off the portside; smaller, white-capped islands off the starboard. On both sides, ice cliffs as high as 500 feet rose out of the water.

In the distance I heard an ominous rumble, like an F-22 fighter racing across the sky. "What's that noise?" I was about to ask our guide, Santi, when he explained it was the sound a glacier makes when it calves into the sea. He had heard it too many times before.

The next morning we prepared to make landfall—at Cuverville Island in the Palmer Archipelago. After we donned our parkas and waterproof pants for our first zodiac (rubber raft) ride to shore, Claudia Roedel, our Brazilian-born expedition leader, made sure we passed inspection. Every pocket, every sleave, every Velcro strip on our clothing was microscopically searched for seeds and plants and any insects that might have stolen away on our voyage. The last step was to swish our company-issued boots through a pan of sanitizing fluid.

"No more than a hundred people are allowed on shore at the same time," Roedel explained. "That's part of the Antarctic Treaty." With our ship's tiny manifest—it wasn't exactly the Queen Mary—we were well within the immigration limit.

A chorus of black-tailed gentoo penguins greeted us when we climbed out of our zodiacs and started up a snowbank. As we drew closer, I realized they weren't singing to us but to each other. "They're calling for their mates," explained Ken Wright, the ship's on-board bird-watcher who doubled as our zodiac driver. "Each call is distinct. Only their partner recognizes it."

I couldn't tell the difference. What I heard was a symphony of warbling bazookas, majestic in their own way. This was nature at its purist. As we listened, two or three members waddled up to us close enough to touch.

"Penguins are intensely curious," Wright said, "and they're not afraid of people. It's because they have no land predators. They have only the leopard seals to be afraid of when they dive for fish."

I wondered how much longer the penguins wouldn't be afraid of us. Each time we encroached on their habitat—even after all our seed and insect inspections—weren't we unwitting accomplices to their eventual extinction? I thought of James Michener's description of Hawaii, which started forming when a stray bird pooped onto the side of a volcano. Except in that instance it created life, it didn't destroy it, which is nature's way.

A few days later, we learned what effect climate change—another human phenomenon—was having on Antarctica's native population. The place was Port Lockroy, a once-abandoned British research station resurrected in 2006 as a museum and—believe it or not—a post office.

Manned by four women, including one recently married who claimed to be on a "solo honeymoon," the station consists of three small buildings perched on a rock off the western shore of Wiencke Island in the Palmer Archipelago.

"We're here for four months and we love every minute of it," one of them said as I paid her for a few postcards. I wondered what these Antarctic women—mostly in their twenties—did for nightlife 8,000 miles away from home at a place where there wasn't any night to begin with, at least in the Antarctic summer.

But what worried me more was the fate of hundreds of not-yet-hatched gentoo chicks that surrounded the rock. While their mothers sat patiently on their eggs, their fathers hunted for stones to build up their nests.

"Their eggs are hatching later than usual this year," said Wright, our Antarctic birdman. "That's because of a late snowfall. Unfortunately, most of the chicks won't survive the winter. They won't be big enough and they'll freeze to death." It was a consequence of climate change I hadn't thought of.

Back onboard the ship, Claudia Roedel, our expedition leader, spoke more about the consequences of climate change—how it's changing Antarctica and how Antarctica, in turn, is changing the world.

"We've entered the Anthropocene," she said, referring to a point-in-time in the earth's geological history where climate change may have a catastrophic effect on life in all its forms.

"The summer of 2022 was the hottest ever," she said. "London had its hottest day on record—104 degrees Fahrenheit. Europe had its worst drought in 500 years. In Pakistan, 500,000 people were flooded out of their homes.

"Here the glaciers are calving off," she said, adding that an iceberg the size of Delaware had broken off Antarctica's Larsen Ice Shelf in July 2017. "The ocean level…is already up about an inch." Roedel added that if all of the Antarctic ice melted, sea levels around the world would rise 200 feet. First, coastal cities like Venice and Miami would go, then Los Angeles and Amsterdam, then San Francisco and Lower

Manhattan. "Without question, humans are the predominant cause of global warming."

So what can we do?

"Switch to clean energy. Reduce our dependence on fossil fuel," Roedel said, citing the use of wind turbines, solar power, LED lights, hybrid cars, nuclear power. "There's no silver bullet, no single solution, but these are things we can do."

Up in the bridge, satellite images on the screens showed another storm moving into the Drake Passage. Our captain, Andrey Rudenko, decided to turn his ship around and get ahead of the storm—something Shackleton surely would have done if he'd had the technology to warn him.

As I looked back at the glaciers, I wondered if Antarctica, a continent we didn't even know existed until 200 years ago, was lashing back for what we were doing to it. Because that was nature's way.

This story is published here for the first time.

Agri, Turkey

Searching for Noah's Ark

LIKE HIS BIBLICAL HERO NOAH who took 120 years to build the ark, Ron Wyatt doesn't give up. The 58-year-old amateur archeologist from Nashville, Tennessee, is determined to prove the sacred vessel landed near Mount Ararat here in eastern Turkey.

Wyatt, who survived a three-week kidnapping ordeal in the region last summer, is back this month to launch a full-scale excavation of a site he first discovered in 1977—a site he's convinced contains the remains of Noah's Ark.

If the boat-shaped formation is indeed the real McCoy, it may well be the century's most important archeological find. The discovery also will have profound implications for millions of religious fundamentalists who will view the find as direct confirmation of the Genesis flood.

Wyatt, himself a fundamentalist, believes God led him to the site. "I just stumbled on it when I was out here exploring with my sons," he said. "I believe the Genesis story is true. My goal now is to convince others."

Winning converts to his cause may be the toughest job of all—not to mention the personal risks of returning to a corner of the world where Westerners aren't especially welcomed. Since beginning his search for the lost ark, the Indiana Jones look-alike has been shot at by terrorists, kidnapped, and jailed as a spy.

Noah's Ark, according to Genesis, landed on Mount Ararat after a 40-day flood. In Turkey the mountain is known as *Agri Dagi*—"Mountain of Pain."

Last summer (1991) was no exception. Seized at a roadblock by Kurdish guerrillas, Wyatt and four members of his party were held hostage for three weeks. The kidnappers later identified themselves as members of the PKK, or Kurdish Labor Party, an outlawed group fighting for an independent state. "They were just looking for attention," Wyatt shrugged. Harried but unharmed, Wyatt and his team were released September 21.

Mount Ararat itself is anything but hospitable. Overlooking the point where the frontiers of Turkey, Iran and the former Soviet republic of Armenia come together, Ararat's 17,000-foot glacier-capped peak rises out of the flat Aras plain like a giant ghost looming over the horizon. Frequent earthquakes and bone-chilling winds make the most intrepid mountain climbers think twice before scaling it. In Turkish the mountain is called *Agri Dagi,* which means "Mountain of Pain."

Ararat is sacred to the few remaining Armenians in the area, who believe they were the first race of humans to appear after the Great Flood. In 1940 an earthquake and avalanche buried an entire village at the spot where, according to local tradition, Noah built an altar and planted the first vineyard. A monastery there once commemorated St. Jacob, who is said to have tried repeatedly but failed to reach the summit in search of the ark.

Wyatt believes St. Jacob was just looking in the wrong place. "There's no doubt in my mind that we've found the ark," he declared, pointing out a 515-foot-long boat-shaped formation far below the summit.

The site itself is located on what the locals call "Doomsday Mountain," a 6,300-foot foothill located 12 miles south of Mount Ararat's peak. Wyatt notes that the geological strata upon which the boat-like formation rests is sedimentary, the type left by a flood.

But more intriguing is the formation's size, which Wyatt says matches exactly the biblical dimensions of the ark. He explains that Moses, thought by most scholars to be the author of Genesis, would have used the ancient Egyptian cubit, 20.62 inches, to describe the ark's size. "The Bible says the ark was 300 cubits long," Wyatt said. "If you multiply that by an Egyptian cubit, that's 515 feet."

Near the slope, a massive wedge-shaped stone juts out from the ground, a six-inch hole carved through the top. Wyatt explains how early seafarers used stones like this to anchor their ships. "We've found a dozen of these scattered in a line about 19 miles long from the northwest. I believe Noah dropped these as he prepared to make landfall."

Wyatt rubs his hand over the surface. "See these carvings?" They're Byzantine crosses, eight of them. Obviously, these were done much later, but each one represents a survivor of the flood—Noah, his wife, and his three sons and their wives."

Wyatt also notes that a village near the ark site is known locally as the Village of Eight. "I've asked the people there how the village got its name and nobody knows." Wyatt believes it refers to the eight survivors.

When Wyatt began his search, he twice sought permission to examine the boat-like object and begin excavations. Both times the Turkish government denied his request. In December 1978 an earthquake opened up a huge crack in the formation, and the following summer the government finally permitted Wyatt to gather oil samples inside the formation.

Galbraith Laboratories in Knoxville analyzed the samples and found distinct differences in the amount of carbon inside the formation compared to samples taken from the surrounding area. Readings of the formation itself revealed significant tracings of petrified wood.

The next step was to survey the site with three types of metal detectors and two subsurface radar systems. Then, on a hot July day in 1985, terrorists attacked. "Turkish intelligence had warned me that this would be a possibility," Wyatt said. "As soon as the attack started, 30 Turkish commandos popped out of nowhere and drove them off with automatic rifles." Before the skirmish was over, three Turkish soldiers and five Iranian terrorists were killed,

Undeterred, Wyatt returned that fall and finished his readings. "We found definable outlines of deck timbers, open chambers and other logical configurations of a very large boat," he said. Wyatt extracted samples of what he described as "decayed and oxidized metal and some partially petrified wood" which he believed was part of a rib timber from the ark.

A radiocarbon analysis at Tennessee's Oak Ridge Laboratories dated the wood at 3740 B.C. Wyatt's own calculations place the flood at 2438 B.C. "This means the timbers were about a thousand years old when Noah started building the ark," he said.

Wyatt's findings prompted Turkish officials to take a closer look. Recently the Turkish government commissioned an archeological team from Ataturk University to conduct its own investigation. But the big dig Wyatt is gearing up for this summer will be far more extensive, involving archeologists from several countries. Whether Wyatt and his team unearth additional evidence of Noah's Ark seems to matter little to Turkish officials. Eager for tourists, they've already opened a visitors center at the site, and giant paving machines line the once dirt road that meanders through the mountains.

WYATT'S CLAIMED DISCOVERY of Noah's Ark is the latest chapter in a long history of quests for the sacred vessel. Since the early 19th century scores of "arkeologists," spurred by shepherds' accounts of a boat-shaped structure protruding from the glacial cap of the mountain, have trooped up its icy slopes. A Russian expedition at the turn of the century claimed to have strolled inside an unfrozen portion of the ark.

In 1948 the discovery of the remains of a petrified ship at the 11,000-foot level of Mount Ararat was reported from Istanbul. British archeologists gained Turkey's consent to explore the site, but when *Pravda,* the Soviet-controlled newspaper in Moscow, accused them of planning espionage, the Turkish government withdrew its consent.

It wasn't until 1959 that Fernard Navarra, a Frenchman, finally got permission to go up the mountain. He returned carrying what he declared were timbers from the vessel, a claim later quashed when radiocarbon dating pegged the wood at about 800 A.D.

In the past 20 years several Americans have joined the search, including the late astronaut James Irwin who made six expeditions to Mount Ararat. Irving, one of 12 astronauts to walk on the moon, returned from his Apollo 15 mission in 1971 with a rock he dubbed the "Genesis Rock," estimated to be 4 billion years old. That discovery made the moon walk a religious experience for him. "I thought the Lord wanted me involved in finding artifacts from the Genesis time that would be more important than the Genesis Rock we found on the moon," he declared. Irwin, who joined Wyatt on two of his expeditions, gave up the search in 1986.

For a time the San Francisco-based Institute for Creation Research had been sending expeditions up the mountain. Led by John Morris, a geological engineer at the University of Oklahoma, the group's expeditions have so far produced two books but no ark. "If indeed there is a boat," explained Morris, "there is only one way it could have gotten up there. That is through a major, global catastrophe that could have restructured the whole surface of the earth."

Indeed, archeological evidence suggests that a great flood did occur—at least in that part of the world. In 1929 a British team led by Sir Leonard Woolley conducted an excavation near the ancient city of Ur, north of the Persian Gulf. Woolley discovered a water-laid deposit some 10 feet thick, dating from the 3rd millennium B.C. The layer, Woolley concluded, represented a solid break in time between civilizations of the Stone and Bronze Ages.

Other excavations were done west of Mount Ararat in the flood plains of the Tigres and Euphrates rivers. Similar evidence was found indicating the two civilizations had been abruptly cut off from each other. The inhabitants had either abandoned the site or suffered a catastrophe that simply wiped all life from the face of their world, leaving only some tools and pottery as proof of their existence.

The archeologists concluded that not even a period of drought or war could have caused such total abandonment. The only possibility was a flood of waters surging out of the Persian Gulf, overflowing the river's banks and whipped into a fury by cyclone-force winds. Careful scrutiny of the traces left by these waters revealed that they had inundated an area estimated at 393 miles by 100 miles. The date: about 3000 B.C.

FEW ARCHEOLOGICAL EXPEDITIONS have had such an explicit goal as the search for Noah's Ark. Wyatt believes his discovery will lead to converts. "Many people who aren't religious might become religious," he said.

But to others, his mission is a quixotic pursuit of the elusive giant. Scoffed New York University archeologist Kenan Erim, noted for his historic finds at Aphrodisias: "There may be something there, but I doubt it. There's too much of religious fundamentalists taking the Bible as literal record. They assume that everything is exactly as it's described in the Bible."

Further complicating Wyatt's claim is that the biblical account of the flood isn't unique. "Many cultures have their own flood traditions," declared Richard Weis, an Old Testament scholar at New Brunswick Theological Seminary. Weis explains that the ancient Babylonians had a flood tradition that predated the Genesis account. It tells the story of a man named Utnapishtim who survived a great flood by building an ark.

In the Babylonian story the destruction resulted from a disagreement among the gods; in Genesis it resulted from moral corruption. The Babylonian flood lasted seven days; the Genesis flood lasted 40. Yet there are so many similarities between the two versions, Weis said, that "there can be no doubt that the Bible borrowed the basic story of the Babylonian account."

Phoenix writer Robert Moore is ready to address Wyatt and other "arkeologists" on their own literal terms. An ex-fundamentalist himself, Moore has published several anti-ark treatises in scientific journals. "There simply could not have been an ark as described in the Bible," he said. Even by grouping similar species together as one kind, the ark would have had to accommodate 3,858,920 animals, he said. "If the dimensions of the craft as laid out in Genesis are accepted, that's a snug one-quarter cubic foot per beast."

Still, respected archeologists like Alpay Pasinli, director of the Istanbul Archeological Museum, isn't ready to rule out Wyatt's claimed discovery. "I think (Noah's Ark) is there," he declared. "I'm an archeologist, a dreamer. An archeologist begins by thinking he's going to find something important. Otherwise, he's just a ditchdigger."

Whatever else Wyatt may find to support his claim, he knows he won't convince everyone. "There are people who still don't believe Jim Irwin walked on the moon."

This story originally appeared in the *Milwaukee Journal,* October 16, 1992.

Xi'an, China

Qin's Terracotta Army

ONE COULD SAY THAT Qin Shi Huang, the first emperor of China, had an ego problem. Qin (pronounced "Chin"), who reigned from 221 to 210 B.C., had no sooner ascended the throne when he ordered 700,000 workers from across his empire to build the world's biggest mausoleum—as a monument to himself.

One could also say that Qin suffered from paranoia, because the next thing he did was order a Great Wall to be built along his domain's northern border to ward off would-be invaders.

Fast forward a few thousand years to March 29, 1974. Central China is struck by drought. A communal orchard shared by inhabitants of a village near the ancient city of Xi'an is drying up.

A 34-year-old farmer named Yang Xinman takes the matter into his own hands. Armed with shovels, pick axes and a divining rod, Yang and two helpers scan the orchard looking for an underground stream.

At a corner of the orchard the divining rod dips down, indicating a likely spot to dig a well. Yang and his helpers jam their shovels into the ground. But the granite-hard clay refuses to yield. They resort to the pick axes to break it up. That afternoon and several yards down, they find broken pieces of pottery but, alas, no water. Exhausted from the effort, they go home.

Interred for more than 2,200 years, these terracotta soldiers were unearthed in 1974 by a farmer digging for water.

Back the next day, they resume digging. After several more hours they find a broken spear and part of an armor. Then they unearth the oddest artifact of all: an earthen head detached from its body. "The opening at the neck was about the size of a bowl," Yang recalled through an interpreter. "I thought we had found an old kiln."

What Yang in fact found turned out to be one of the greatest archaeological discoveries of modern times. Near the tomb of China's first emperor lay an extraordinary treasure: an army of life-size terracotta soldiers and horses interred for more than 2,200 years. Their purpose: to protect the emperor in his afterlife.

So far 8,000 soldiers have been unearthed, in addition to scores of horses and war chariots. Each soldier is life-size and unique, down to the facial features. Even their armors and hairstyles are distinct, indicating their military rank.

A 3½-acre field house, built for protection against the weather and pollution from nearby Xi'an, covers the biggest pit containing 6,000 soldiers. Another pit contains cavalry and infantry units. Still another contains high ranking officers and chariots. A fourth pit lies empty, suggesting the workers packed up and went home after the emperor died. A museum and visitor center complete the 35-acre complex.

As for the emperor's tomb, less than one percent has been excavated so far because of mercury found in the burial mound, which archaeologists believe the emperor used to simulate rivers coursing through his tomb.

In 2011 the museum launched two long-term excavations of the mound, yielding a circus of terracotta acrobats and strong men. Wu Yongqi, the museum's director, predicts more "mind-boggling discoveries" as the excavations continue.

In 1987 the United Nations declared the terracotta army a UNESCO World Heritage Site. Former French President Jacques Chirac called it the "eighth wonder of the world." Last year it drew more than a million visitors.

Meanwhile, Yang, now 74, the farmer who started the whole fuss, sits quietly in a corner of the museum signing books about his find and posing for pictures. "When the museum opened, I couldn't afford a ticket," he said. "They agreed to let me in if I signed books."

It's a good deal for both. "People buy these books and I sign them," he said, displaying his John Hancock-like signature in Chinese. He charges 20 yuan ($3.25) to have his picture taken. Then he adds with a sly grin: "I make more money now than I did as a farmer."

This story first appeared in the *Detroit Free Press*, March 23, 2014.

Svirstroy, Russia

Russia's Inside Passage

ON THE BANK OF THE SVIR RIVER, one hundred and sixty miles northeast of St. Petersburg, lies a village so remote you won't find it on Wikipedia. Yet it symbolizes as much as anyplace in this vast land a nation struggling to reinvent itself after communism.

An eight-year-old named Peter—presumably after the great Russian czar who made the river navigable from the outside world—greeted passengers from the *M.S. Rossia* with bicycle tricks, a kitten clinging to his shoulder.

When he finished his routine he held out a crocheted egg warmer to his audience of bystanders. "You buy?" he said in broken English. "My mother make it."

"How much?" I asked.

"A hundred rubles," Peter replied.

Forgetting to bargain, I paid the boy his asking price—about $3. The transaction drew stares from adult vendors hawking goods of their own, everything from woolen scarves and fur hats to carved wooden plates and hand-painted *matryoshka* dolls.

"This ship and its sister, the *M.S. Tikhi Don,* support the economy of this town," said Jenia Beralinova, our guide. "There aren't many jobs here, so they need all the help they can get."

Every other week, between May and October, the two ships cross each other on the Russian waterways, a 1,143-mile

Worshippers celebrate the 300th anniversary of the Church of the Transfiguration on Kizhi Island, August 19, 2014.

stretch between St. Petersburg and Moscow, making Svirstroy their first or last port-of-call, depending on which direction they're going. The route covers four rivers, three lakes (including the two largest in Europe, Ladoga and Onega), two canals, a reservoir, and sixteen locks.

Besides Russia's two major cities, the cruise includes stopovers in Petrozavodsk, a city on Lake Onega; a visit to a 14th century monastery in Goritsy, and a walking tour of the ancient town of Uglich, where the murder of a prince ushered in the Romanov dynasty 400 years ago.

It also takes in what may be the most isolated UNESCO World Heritage site in the world—the centuries-old wood-domed Church of the Transfiguration on Kizhi Island, three hundred miles from the Arctic Circle. Off-season, the island's twenty residents depend on weekly helicopter drops for their provisions.

Petrozavodsk (population 260,000), on Lake Onega's western shore, appears frozen in a Soviet time warp. A statue of Lenin presides over the town square. A rusted-out trolley stops to pick up passengers. On the lakefront two wire-sculptured fishermen cast their nets into the water—a gift from Petrozavodsk's sister city, Duluth, Minnesota.

It's a nice touch. But when it comes to economic help, there's only so much a sister can do. "Unemployment here is 30 percent," complained Andrei Rysakov, an English teacher. "All the young people go to Moscow or St. Petersburg because that's where the jobs are. In the rural areas unemployment is more like 60 percent."

Which brings us back to Svirstroy. With 600 inhabitants the town is a shadow of what it used to be. Abandoned buildings dot the landscape. A tiny Russian orthodox church with room for about 10 worshipers stands a few hundred feet from the riverbank.

Jenia, our guide, led a group from the *M.S. Rossia* to a modest frame house next to a garden patch. At the front door she introduced us to Elena, age 60-something, who invited us in for tea and stuffed pastries called *piroshki,* a specialty of the region.

I studied Elena's face as she poured the tea from her *samovar,* a Russian contraption that seemed a bit complicated for the task. The wistfulness in her eyes betrayed her smile as she talked about better times.

"I lost my life savings when everything in Russia changed," she said, Jenia interpreting for her. "My government pension is 6,000 rubles a month ($180), so I live here with my daughter and her husband to keep expenses down."

Jenia added that Elena, like other pensioners in Svirstroy, was "paid by the company" for entertaining her American visitors. Based on the size of our group and the number of passengers on our ship, I calculated that a dozen visits like this were taking place. Talk about supporting the town's economy.

Later I asked Jenia what Elena meant when she said "everything in Russia changed."

"When (former President Boris) Yeltsin freed the ruble from state control, it wiped out millions of people's savings," she said. "All the stress affected people's health. Did you know the average life expectancy in Russia is the lowest among industrialized nations?"

I wondered if the average Russian was any better off under Joseph Stalin, who ran the country with an iron fist from 1922 to 1953. He caused his share of stress, too, when he sent millions of people off to the gulags of Siberia.

At Uglich we learned that life for the average Russian wasn't any better under the czars. Ivan the Terrible, who reigned from 1533 to 1584, routinely killed off princes and nobles who posed a threat to him. In 1581 he murdered his own son in a fit of rage, leaving as his successor 8-year-old Prince Dmitry, who himself came to an untimely end. Just how, nobody knows for sure. But most fingers point to Boris Godunov, a minor prince, as the culprit. The Church of St. Dmitry (1692) marks the spot where the young lad died.

So is the average Russian any better off today?

Ask Evgeny Zalman's 80-year-old grandmother and she'll tell you, "Life is more stable now. I wake up in the same country I went to sleep in."

That's why she likes Russian President Vladimir Putin. But ask her 28-year-old grandson, and he'll give you a different answer. "I don't trust him," Evgeny said, admitting he voted for Putin in 2012 in an election widely suspected of being rigged. "I had little choice. The other candidates were clowns."

So is he free to speak his mind?

"More so than my parents or grandparents," he said. "My generation values freedom of speech above everything else. But I'm careful what I say in public."

Meanwhile that other nemesis of the once evil empire—capitalism—is alive and well, at least in Moscow. I watched as hordes of customers lined up at a new McDonald's near the Kremlin. And the next time I go back—who knows?—I might find Peter, my young entrepreneur friend from Svirstroy, hawking a Mercedes on television.

This story first appeared in the *Chicago Tribune*, January 20, 2013.

Mont-Saint-Michel, France

Enduring the Sands of Time

TO A VISITOR APPROACHING from the east on a late summer afternoon, Mont-Saint-Michel rises from the sand like a giant shadowy pyramid. Sitting inexplicably off the Normandy coast of France, it is in fact a solitary hunk of granite with a monastery on top.

For more than 1,200 years it has been visited by pilgrims and tourists alike. Anyone who makes the 250-foot climb to the summit, whether to pray or ponder the mystery of how it got there, cannot help but marvel at this joint handiwork of God and man.

Ever since the dark ages, ferocious tides surged into the bay twice a day and turned the rock that once stood in the middle of a forest into a majestic island. But now, after a century of mankind's meddling with nearby rivers and dikes, the bay is clogged with sand, the tides have lost their oomph, and Mont-Saint-Michel is becoming high and dry. Yet today it remains one of France's premier tourist attractions.

The mount has been surrounded by magic and myth since 708 A.D. when the Archangel Michel, according to tradition, appeared in a vision to Saint Aubert, the bishop of nearly Avranches, and commanded him to build a shrine on

In Mont-Saint-Michel's world of sculpted stone, the work of God and man is joined together.

top of the rock. Mount Tombe, as it was then called, was surrounded by the Scissy forest.

In the 11th century, long after the tides swept away the forest, Benedictine monks built a spectacular Romanesque church out of the native granite. In the 13th century they added an elegant Gothic monastery that still adorns the pinnacle of the mount.

The tides and surrounding quicksand made the island fortress too tough for the English to conquer during the One Hundred Years' War (1337-1453). Recognizing that it was just as difficult to get to shore, French revolutionaries converted it into a prison, a la Alcatraz, in 1789. Among its inmates: the writers Dubourg and Desforges.

Today the tides, which vary as much as 35 feet, are still the greatest along the French coast, but that's not enough to satisfy Father Bruno de Senneville, who presides over the monastery. Declares the Benedictine monk with a businessman's instinct: "If there were higher tides, there would be more tourists."

In 1982 a Paris-based engineer, Jean Doulcier, came up with a solution: Destroy a dike two miles away that would allow the Selune and See rivers to resume their natural courses into Mont-Saint-Michel Bay. In addition, build reservoirs, floodgates and locks to hold back the water, then release it in a flood to wash the sand out to sea.

Not everyone bought the idea, especially when they learned there was a $40 million price tag attached to the project. Bemoans Father Bruno: "People can't seem to accept that beauty on this earth is not a cheap commodity."

Whether mankind's meddling will ever be undone remains to be seen, but more than a million tourists a year still come to this solitary island to be cast under its spell.

Girdled by ramparts and towers, Mont-Saint-Michel's granite rock boasts a year-round population of 114, most of whom inhabit the medieval town along its base. The only entrance is through the Avancee Gate that stands at the end of a one-mile causeway leading out from the mainland shore.

The Grand Rue, a narrow street lined with souvenir shops, restaurants and hotels, winds up the mount to the monastery and abbey church.

It there's one event visitors who make the pilgrimage don't want to miss, it's the annual feast of the Archangel Michel, held in early autumn. The festival enjoys a centuries-old tradition that, befitting the island's patron saint, climaxes the merrymaking with a solemn mass in the abbey church in which, it is hoped, everyone's overindulgence will be forgiven.

The island also features an historical museum with wax figures and dioramas that evoke scenes of dungeon horrors from the abbey's stint as a prison.

The best way to get to Mont-Sant-Michel is by car. It's a three-hour drive from Paris, and parking is available along the causeway. But when you leave your car, be prepared to step back centuries in time. As you proceed up the winding Grand Rue to the top of the mount, the surrounding view of the tidal flats and Normandy coastline will leave an indelible impression. For in this world of sculpted stone, where the work of God and man is joined together, the mortal visitor discovers he is at one with nature.

This story first appeared in the Springfield (Illinois) *State Journal-Register*, October 20, 1985.

Dyersville, Iowa

Finding Heaven in a Cornfield

JUST OUTSIDE THIS LITTLE farming town in northeast Iowa lies a baseball field where dreams refuse to die. When Universal Studios took over Don Lansing's farm and turned it into a movie set for the 1989 hit film "Field of Dreams," it became the hottest tourist attraction in the history of Dubuque County.

Today the Hollywood film crews are long gone and the farmers are back to growing corn. Still, like the movie says, the people will come.

And come they do. An estimated 10,000 visitors will have made the pilgrimage before summer's out.

"This field is really like a shrine," said Lansing, an amiable 47-year-old bachelor whose farm has been in the family for three generations. "It's amazing. There was an 80-year-old man out here the other day pitching to his grandson."

Lansing presides benignly over it all, patiently answering visitors' questions and pointing out things like the heart that actor Kevin Costner carved in the first-base bleachers with the words "Ray loves Annie." (Costner played Ray Kinsella in the film, while Amy Madigan played his wife Annie.)

Top: Don Lansing presides benignly over the baseball field at his farm, site of the 1989 hit film "Field of Dreams." Bottom: Chicago White Sox and New York Yankees players step out of the corn to play out their dreams, August 21, 2021. (The White Sox won, 9-8.)

Lansing admits that the movie "has pretty much changed my life," but he clearly enjoys his new-found celebrity status, not to mention the improvements the film's construction crew made on his farm.

He motions to his house near first base. "They added the veranda and hung a swing there. They put in all new windows and hardwood floors, an open staircase, and even central air conditioning. Not bad for a 90-year-old farmhouse."

Yet Lansing refuses to take advantage of his visitors. They can buy a "Field of Dreams" sweatshirt from his makeshift souvenir stand or drop a few quarters into the soft-drink machine.

It took four months during the summer of 1988 to make the film. For Lansing, the highlight was the climactic scene in which 1,500 cars formed a three-mile procession from Dyersville to his farm.

"Everyone gathered at the park for hot dogs and potato chips," he said. "Then they all lined up at 4 o'clock and started out at dusk with their headlights on. It was spectacular."

Visitors to Lansing's farm are getting a slightly different view of the baseball field than they saw in the movie. A telephone line now stretches across third base to right field.

"Over there, that belongs to my neighbors, Al and Rita Ameskamp," said Lansing, pointing to left field. For now, the field is plowed under. Just behind third base, the Ameskamps have put up a mailbox that reads: "Keep left field alive." A slit at the top invites donations.

Behind the backstop, Lansing has his own contributions box to help maintain the infield. "It's no big deal," he said. "Still, between the neighbors and me, we're losing about 3½ acres of corn to keep this field."

So why not charge admission?

"I wouldn't think of it," Lansing says. "It was just an honor to have my farm selected. I'm not going to take it away from the people."

A plastic bat and whiffleball lay between first base and the pitcher's mound. A teen-ager picked up the ball and called to his father, "Dad, let's play catch."

Lansing smiled. "That's what this place is all about."

This story first appeared in the *Los Angeles Times*, September 2, 1990.

Part Two: People

Virginia Dare

America's First Missing Child

MANTEO, N.C. (August 18, 1987)—In a place where American history is measured in centuries, today marks a milestone: Virginia Dare was born here on Roanoke Island on August 18, 1587—exactly 400 years ago. She was the first English child born in America and the epicenter of America's first great mystery.

Not yet 3 years old when she dropped out of sight, Virginia Dare was one of a group of New World pioneers who became known as the Lost Colony.

Sent by Sir Walter Raleigh to colonize the New World, they set up shop on Roanoke Island on the Outer Banks of what is now North Carolina. Their arrival in the summer of 1587, 200 years before the U.S. Constitution was drafted in Philadelphia, marked what one historian calls "the spiritual beginning of America."

Yet all 118 of them vanished, leaving only the word "CROATOAN" carved on a tree. Since then countless explorations, excavations and genealogical searches have failed to turn up any confirmed trace of the legendary Lost Colony.

Historians generally concede the mystery will never be solved, but the spirit of Virginia Dare and the other colonists lives on. It still has enough power to inspire archeologists to

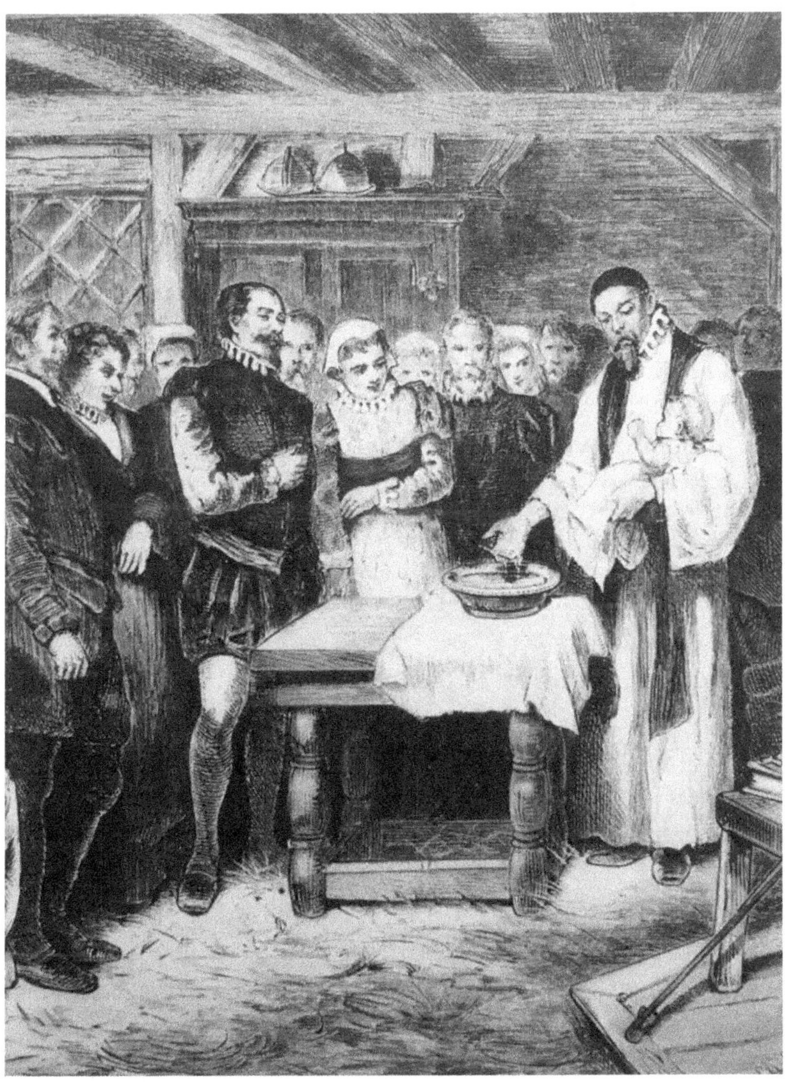

Within three years of her christening in the New World, Virginia Dare was gone.

keep digging for artifacts that might provide a clue, to keep historians sifting through old records, to draw tourists to a drama about the Lost Colony that boasts a 50-year run.

ADOLPH DIAL, 64, a Lumbee Indian who heads the Department of Indian Studies at Pembroke State University in Pembroke, N.C., has an interest in the matter that's more than academic: He's convinced that the Lost Colonists are the ancestors of his 36,000 fellow Lumbees living in what is now Robeson County in southeastern North Carolina.

And he believes that he himself is a descendant of Virginia Dare.

Precious few details are known about the colony's most famous citizen. Twenty-seven days after the settlers arrived, she was born to Ananias and Eleanor Dare, who was the daughter of the colony's governor. On Aug. 24 she was christened "Virginia" after the "virgin queen," Elizabeth I. Less than three years later—nobody knows exactly when—the colony vanished.

"The oral tradition is clear that Virginia Dare's family survived and that the Dials in Robeson County are her descendants," Dial said in a flat, almost Old English drawl. "Even today, if you pronounce Dare with the accent people speak here, it sounds very much like Dial."

Admittedly, to a casual listener from the North, the two names come out sounding pretty much alike.

"Not only that," Dial continued, "there are at least 41 names of the lost colonists that are still among our people here in Robeson County—names like Brooks, Berry and Jones."

Dial said the carving on the tree is the key that unlocks the mystery of the Lost Colony. Five weeks after the settlers arrived, they persuaded their governor, John White, to go back to England to get provisions.

Before White left, he instructed those who remained to signal their whereabouts in case they moved away. They were to carve the name of their new location on a tree. If they left because of some danger, such as an attack by the Indians or the Spanish, they were to add a Maltese cross as a sign of distress

As it turned out, it took White three years to return to Roanoke because all of England's ships were pressed into service against the Spanish Armada. When he finally returned on Aug. 18, 1590—his granddaughter's third birthday—White found the island deserted: no settlers, no Indians. Buried chests had been dug up and broken open. On a tree near the site he found the word "CROATOAN." There was no Maltese cross.

Croatoan was the village of Manteo, an Algonquian Indian who had befriended the colonists. Dial believes that when John White found the carving, he took it to mean the colonists moved to Manteo's village, about 50 miles to the south, near Cape Hatteras.

White never did find them. Back aboard ship, a severe storm prompted the captain, Abraham Cooke, to pull anchor. He meant to sail south and land White at Croatoan, but once clear of the Outer Banks, the ship rode the winds of the storm for days until it was too far out in the Atlantic to return. Cooke set a new course for the Azores, and White, heartbroken, took a last lingering look over the west horizon. He never saw his granddaughter or the other colonists after that.

Dial speculates that the colonists intermarried with Manteo's people, moved inland, assimilated with other tribes, and eventually settled into what is now Robeson County.

Apparently, all contact with the settlers' descendants was lost until 1660, when an adventurer named Morgan Jones walked across the Carolinas and was captured and then befriended by Indians who spoke English.

"His descriptions suggest that he was in the area of Robeson County," Dial said, but he added that the only record of Jones' letter was a newspaper account of it published in 1840 in the *Charleston Gazette*.

In the 1730s, the first big wave of Scottish immigrants reached the Cape Fear Valley. "When they arrived, they were astonished to find a group of English-speaking people already living there in European-type homes and tilling the soil in European fashion. Many of them were blue-eyes and blond-haired, just like many of the Lumbees today."

Through the centuries, Dial claimed, the two cultures had integrated so completely that they developed extraordinary speech patterns, passing along the English language in a form that was spoken in the 16th century.

"I don't know it to be a fact," Dial said, "but I firmly believe the descendants of the Lost Colony are right here in Robeson County. If I were a betting man, I'd give it all kinds of odds."

But other historians hold other views. David Stick, an Outer Banks resident and author of *Roanake Island: The Beginnings of British America,* believes the settlers split in two or three directions after leaving Roanoke. But he said speculation over their fate obscures "the more important fact" that their colonization effort helped pave the way for the successful settlement of Jamestown, Virginia, two decades later.

"The fact that Raleigh's people established their claim in the name of Elizabeth, built a fort and houses and opened a discourse with the natives, gave notice that England intended to stay Spain's northward occupation of the American mainland.

David Beers Quinn, recognized by most authorities as the dean of Roanoke scholars, believes that most of the settlers made their way to the Elizabeth River near Chesapeake Bay and were massacred there by Powhatan, another Algonquian, in 1607, the same year as the settlement at Jamestown.

Explained Quinn: When John Smith, the governor of Jamestown, sent an expedition in 1608 to look for the lost colonists, his men came back with reports of how "men, women and children of the first plantation at Roanoke were… miserably slaughtered."

"There's no doubt," concluded Quinn, now professor emeritus of history at the University of Liverpool in England, "that Powhatan was held responsible for the violent and bloody end of the Lost Colony."

Other reports obtained by the Jamestown expedition suggest that survivors of Powhatan's massacre found their way to Chowanoke, an ancient Indian capital on the Chowan River about 80 miles inland from Roanoke Island.

"Our problem is access," complained anthropologist David Phelps, who began excavating the area three years ago. Resort cottages and private farms now occupy much of a half-mile stretch from along the Chowan River where the Indian town once stood.

Phelps, who teaches at East Carolina University in Greenville, North Carolina, explained that carbon dating indicates that the town site was occupied from about 825 to 1640 A.D., "but so far we haven't found any artifacts that relate to the 1587 colony. That might change if we could dig in a few front yards."

Two other recent excavations, one at Hatteras Island, believed to be the site of Croatoan, and one at Roanoke itself, have been just as fruitless. "We tested the sands at Hatteras in 1983 and found some animal bones, stone tools, arrow points and bits of pottery, but that was all," Phelps said.

In 1985 archeologists from the Southeast Archeological Center, a National Park Service unit based in Tallahassee, Florida, dug in at Roanoke near the site of a fortress built by Ralph Lane on an expedition to the Outer Banks in 1585. Aerial photos had shown possible signs of a second fortified area near the reconstructed Lane fortress at what is now the Fort Raleigh National Historic Site.

"We had hoped to find some remains of the 1597 colony," Philip Evans, a park service historian at Fort Raleigh said with a sigh, "but all we found were the remains of a dirt road built in the 1920s."

VIRGINIA DARE'S 350th birthday in 1937 opened another fascinating chapter in the long saga of the Lost Colony. That year marked the premiere performance of Paul Greene's outdoor drama, "The Lost Colony," at Fort Raleigh. Today, 50 years later, it's still going strong.

Coincidentally, that same year, a man named L.E. Hammond showed up at Emory University in Atlanta with a peculiar-looking rock. Hammond said he had found it in a North Carolina swamp. Something was written on it, but he couldn't make out the words. Haywood Pearce Jr., a professor of history at Emory, went to work on it. The inscription read: "Ananias Dare and Virginia went hence into heaven 1591."

The stone was either a priceless historical find or a brazen hoax. Meanwhile, Pearce began deciphering a much longer message carved on the other side of the stone. It wasn't an easy task; the inscriptions were faint, and the Elizabethan words were hard to translate.

Finally the message was decoded, and it was a historian's dream. Signed with the initials of Eleanor White Dare, the stone sketched a story of "misarie & Warre" and told how "salvages" had killed all but seven of the colonists and buried 17 of them on a nearby hill.

Sensing that a major discovery was in their grasp, Pearce and other Emory scholars persuaded Hammond to lead them to the place where the stone was found. Hammond took them to a swamp along the Chowan River near the site of Chowanoke, the ancient Indian capital. They searched but found nothing more.

Meanwhile, Harvard University historian Samuel Eliot Morison was called into the case. Incredibly, he pronounced the stone a genuine relic of the Elizabethan age. Soon more stones were discovered near the town of Pelzer, South Carolina, and along the Chattahoochee River in Hall County, Georgia, each one adding precious details to the story: "Father wee go sw…Father brynge you hither…Father the salvage shew moche mercye…."

By now even Cecil B. DeMille had got wind of the discoveries and was said to be considering an epic movie about the Lost Colony mystery. In all, 27 stones turned up, each one duly surrendered for the inspection of eager historians.

But then the bubble burst. Intrigued by a manuscript submitted by Pearce, the *Saturday Evening Post* sent a reporter named Boyden Sparkes to investigate the story. Sparkes' inquiries revealed a morass of contradictions and coincidences that eventually pointed the finger of fraud at the stonemason who had made and reported the find in the first place.

WHILE THE FATE of Virginia Dare and her fellow colonists remains a mystery, attempts to trace her family roots have been a shade more successful.

Virginia's parents, Ananias Dare and Eleanor White, are believed to have been married in London at St. Bride's Church on Fleet Street. Today, as it did 400 years ago, is stands almost in the shadow of St. Paul's Cathedral.

In 1957 a terra cotta effigy of Virginia Dare noting her St. Bride's connection was unveiled there and is still on display.

"We're almost certain her parents were married here, but we don't know the date," said St. Bride's rector John Oates. "The parish records show they were members here and so was Eleanor's father, John White."

White, the colony's governor, was a member of the Painters and Stainer's Guild of London. (His drawings and watercolors done on an earlier voyage to America, in 1585, comprise a superb record of the Algonquin Indians and are displayed to this day at the British Museum.)

St. Bride's records of baptisms, marriages and burials go back, coincidentally, to only 1587, the year the colonists left for America. But the records show burial dates of four "John White" children, two sons and two daughters, who died between 1593 and 1596.

Assuming their father was the same John White who governed the 1587 colony, they would have been Virginia Dare's aunts and uncles. The proximity of their deaths suggests the possibility they perished in the Great London Plague of the 1590s.

There is no record of John White's death. Indeed, after his last futile voyage to America in 1590 to find the Roanoke colony, he seems to have dropped out of sight.

As for Ananias Dare, the record is even more obscure. During an extended visit to England in 1957, historian William Powell of the University of North Carolina found evidence suggesting that Virginia's father came originally from Essex or Devonshire, but it was inconclusive.

Powell's most interesting find was that Ananias Dare fathered a son out of wedlock who stayed behind in England. "His name was John Dare," Powell reported. "The name of his mother appears not to be recorded. He was, nevertheless, acknowledged by his father and bore the name Dare."

Under English law, Powell explained, an unaccounted-for absence of seven years was necessary for a ruling of presumed death. In 1594, a relative of young John Dare's petitioned the court that John be given his father's property. In 1597, seven years after his father sailed to England for the last time, the court granted the son's petition.

Speculation about why Virginia Dare's parents made the voyage to America in the first place is no less intriguing than the mystery of their disappearance. Was it because John White wanted his pregnant daughter to join him as an encouragement to other prospective colonists? Was it because Ananias Dare wanted to escape the stigma of his having fathered a child out of wedlock? Was it because Sir Walter Raleigh promised 500 acres to the head of each household who signed up?

Whatever the reasons, Ananias Dare and his pregnant wife left London to set sail from Plymouth, England, on May 8, 1587, and seek their fortune in America. That same year another Englishman of their generation, a budding 23-year-old playwright named William Shakespeare, arrived from Stratford-on-Avon to seek his fortune in London.

THE SEARCH GOES ON. Where Virginia Dare and her compatriots finally ended up is still anybody's guess, but historians generally agree on these possibilities:

When the colonists left Roanoke Island or Croatoan, some of them moved inland, perhaps splitting into two or more groups.

Some may have wound up in Robeson County, but it's more likely they went to Chowanoke or the Elizabeth River near Chesapeake Bay.

Powhatan almost certainly slaughtered some of the colonists. But it was the general practice among the Indians to spare the women and children, and some men may have escaped as well.

Some of the colonists may still have been alive and living with friendly Indians when the Jamestown settlers arrived in 1607.

Like his claimed forebears who stood courageously alone in the American wilderness, Adolph Dial holds fast to his conviction that the lost colonists wound up in Robeson County. Yet as long as inquisitive people dig holes in the ground and search through moldy records of times past, the search will continue.

Despite their differences over what happened to Virginia Dare and those earliest of American pioneers, Dial and his fellow historians agree on one point: Raleigh's attempt to establish a colony in North America served notice to Spain that England was here to stay.

Declared John Neville, executive director of America's 400th Anniversary celebration: "Many people don't think the Lost Colonists were important. But they were the first English-speaking people to arrive on our shores, and that was the spiritual beginning of America."

This story originally appeared in the *Chicago Tribune*, August 18, 1987.

Thomas Jefferson

The Reluctant Revolutionary

PHILADELPHIA—At nine o'clock Thursday morning, July 4, 1776, Thomas Jefferson looked out the second-floor window of his apartment at Seventh and Market Streets, noted that his thermometer registered 72½ degrees, and set out for the Pennsylvania State House a few blocks away.

No one, least of all Virginia's 33-year-old delegate to the Continental Congress, knew this was going to be the most important day of his life. He stopped to browse at an open-air shop on Market Street, picked out seven pairs of women's gloves, and paid the shopkeeper 27 shillings, noting the price in his pocket account book.

Jefferson's thoughts were more on home—specifically his wife, Martha—than on politics that morning. And had he any choice in the matter, he would have chosen to be home at her bedside, not in Philadelphia to be midwife at a nation's birth.

Only a few of Jefferson's colleagues in the Congress knew how ill she was. Yet his anxiety was so great that he had written a letter some weeks before that nearly cancelled his rendezvous with world history.

Although the letter is lost, we know from references to it that he had urged his neighbor, Dr. George Gilmer, Albemarle

This portrait of Thomas Jefferson was painted in 1786, four years after his wife died. You can still see the depression in his eyes.

County's representative at the Virginia convention meeting in Williamsburg, to find a replacement for him in the Congress.

Unable to attend, Gilmer passed the request on to another friend, Edmund Randolph, whose efforts on Jefferson's behalf were roundly rebuffed. "I urged it in decent terms," Randolph wrote Jefferson on June 23, "but stirred up a swarm of wasps about my ears, who seemed suspicious that I designed to prejudice you."

And so with an irony that seems to be history's favorite sport, Jefferson remained at his desk in Philadelphia, fretting daily over Martha, not knowing in fact whether she was even alive.

To this day Martha Jefferson—called Patty by her family—remains a mystery. No portrait of her is known to exist. The family tradition is that she was beautiful but frail, with radiant auburn hair and large hazel eyes. She was a widow of 23 when Jefferson married her on New Year's Day, 1772.

Yet of all the correspondence he amassed in his lifetime—some 18,000 of his letters have been preserved—not one has been found that he sent to her or she to him. The likelihood is that Jefferson destroyed this highly personal correspondence. As historian Dumas Malone put it: "His wife did not belong to posterity; she belonged to him."

ANYONE FAMILIAR with Jefferson's domestic life during those hot, historic days in Philadelphia could hardly blame him for wanting to go home. This was his third stint in the Congress in 13 months. He had first come in June 1775 as an alternate to his cousin, Peyton Randolph, only to return home in September to find his 18-month-old daughter, Jane, gravely ill. Though he and Martha tried desperately to nurse her back to health, she died a few weeks later, leaving an older sister, Martha, age 3.

Meanwhile, the Virginia Convention had just elected Jefferson a delegate in his own right, and the Congress was preparing to reconvene. Already delayed by Jane's death, he left his wife with her sister and brother-in-law at a place called The Forest, near Richmond, and hurried on to Philadelphia. At least he knew she was in good hands.

But two weeks passed, then a month. Jefferson heard nothing. Finally on November 7 he fired off a frantic letter to Martha's brother-in-law, Francis Eppes: "The suspense under which I am is too terrible to be endured. If anything has happened, for God's sake let me know it."

With all-out war a virtual certainty, the Congress abandoned its plans to adjourn in late December. As for Jefferson, he had had enough of anxiety, and on December 28 he left Philadelphia and headed home.

Back at Monticello, he spent the next four months in seclusion. Not a single letter of his is recorded between December 10, 1775, and May 16, 1976, nor are there references to any. His Garden Book, in which he otherwise meticulously recorded every planting at Monticello, is also blank during this period, though he was home during the peak of spring planting.

Jefferson apparently did little but care for Martha during those months. Why she was ill no one knows for sure. Some believe she was diabetic, but the evidence is scanty. Chances are she was pregnant. Of six Jefferson children, only two survived infancy, and there may have been other pregnancies that ended in miscarriage.

In February Jefferson received a letter from his friend and fellow delegate in Philadelphia, Thomas Nelson, who had taken his wife with him. "You must certainly bring Mrs. Jefferson with you," Nelson urged, adding that his wife would "take all possible care of her."

Jefferson agonized over what to do. Duty demanded that he return to the Congress. But Martha was in no condition to make the seven-day trip over dirt roads and bridgeless rivers, to say nothing of the miasmatic night air and the other health hazards to which she would be exposed in Philadelphia. And he was not about to leave her alone.

During this period another tragedy occurred. On March 31 Jefferson wrote in his account book: "My mother died about 8 o'clock this morning, in the 57th year of her age." She was the victim of an apoplectic stroke, and though all her children were grown, her death no doubt added to her son Thomas's mental burden.

Right after this Jefferson suffered a blinding, debilitating headache—what we now call a migraine—that persisted for the next six weeks. A few of Jefferson's biographers have linked it to his mother's death, but one of them, Thomas Fleming, suggests another cause: "Jefferson had planned to leave for Philadelphia at the end of March; one might think that the attack was brought on by an unconscious desire to find some excuse, no matter how tortuous, to delay his departure."

Finally, by May 7, he was over it. He took out his account book, wrote "Left with Mrs. Jefferson £10," and set out for Philadelphia for the last time.

Meanwhile, an ex-London corset-maker named Thomas Paine exploded into print with a pamphlet titled *Common Sense*. Condemning George III as "the greatest enemy this continent hath," he issued a loud, fervent call for independence. "The sun never shined on a cause of greater worth," he cried. "The blood of the slain, the weeping voice of nature, cries, 'TIS TIME TO PART.'"

Paine's message spread through the colonies like wildfire. When Jefferson arrived in Philadelphia, he found a letter from his friend John Page: "For God's sake, declare the colonies independent at once, and save us from ruin."

All Jefferson could do was wait. The Virginia Convention was scheduled to meet in Williamsburg on May 15, and without instructions from home, the delegates in Philadelphia could do nothing. To pass the time he took up another project that he deemed just as important back home: writing a new state constitution for Virginia.

Jefferson was in Philadelphia only three days when his worries about Martha resurfaced. On May 16 he wrote to

Nelson, now back in Virginia: "I am here in the same uneasy, anxious state in which I was the last fall without Mrs. Jefferson, who could not come with me."

In spite of his anxiety, or perhaps because of it, he forged ahead on the new Virginia constitution. A few weeks later it was finished, ready to be sent to Williamsburg.

Meanwhile the long-awaited instructions arrived from the Virginia Convention, and on Friday, June 7, Richard Henry Lee stood up in the assembly room to read his historic resolution: "That these united colonies are and of right ought to be free and independent states, that they are absolved from all allegiance to the British crown, and that all connection between them and the State of Great Britain is, and ought to be, totally dissolved."

Debate was postponed until the following day. At 10 o'clock Saturday morning the delegates reassembled. The radicals, led by Lee and John Adams, argued ferociously with John Dickinson and James Wilson of Pennsylvania, Robert Livingston of New York, and Edward Rutledge of South Carolina.

The issue narrowed to one of timing. The middle colonies were not yet ripe for the break. Better to wait, they argued, than to force the issue and risk succession. To this the radicals replied that independence was already a fact, that a declaration would merely acknowledge it.

The debate rumbled into the night with no end in sight. Finally, on Monday, June 10, the two sides reached a compromise: postpone the vote for three more weeks. This would give the middle colonies time to write their assemblies for instructions. But just in case, appoint a committee at once to draw up a formal declaration of independence. The committee chosen: Thomas Jefferson of Virginia, John Adams of Massachusetts, Benjamin Franklin of Pennsylvania, Roger Sherman of Connecticut, and Robert Livingston of New York.

Who was to write it? Franklin was confined to a friend's home outside of town with an attack of the gout, and neither Sherman nor Livingston had any literary reputation, so the choice came down to Adams and Jefferson. Years later Adams described how Jefferson urged the job on him, but he declined.

"Why will you not?" Jefferson asked. "You ought to do it."

"I will not."

"Why?"

"Reasons enough."

"What can be your reasons?"

"Reason first, you are a Virginian, and a Virginian ought to appear at the head of this business. Reason second, I am obnoxious, suspected, and unpopular. You are very much otherwise. Reason third, you can write 10 times better than I can."

Jefferson went to work. For the next 17 days, before and after the business hours of Congress, he labored over his writing box. His quill scratched tirelessly, carving and polishing the words. He wrote in a fine, clear, meticulous script, aware that each word counted.

That Lee's resolution for independence would pass he had little doubt. His job was to give it a philosophical foundation. As a result, the ideas he so carefully forged into words were not his alone, they were universal. Thus he began:

"When in the course of human events it becomes necessary for one people to dissolve the political bands which have connected them with another, and to assume among the powers of the earth the separate and equal station to which the laws of nature and nature's God entitle them, a decent respect to the opinions of mankind requires that they declare the causes which impel them to the separation.

"We hold these truths to be sacred and undeniable," he continued, "that all men are created equal, that they are endowed by their creator with certain inalienable rights, that among these are life, liberty, and the pursuit of happiness...."

The sentiments belonged to mankind. Later Jefferson said his purpose was "not to find out new principles, or new arguments, never before thought of...but to place before mankind the common sense of the subject....It was intended to be an expression of the American mind."

Yet even as he wrote, he had a lurking sense that he was risking, perhaps even sacrificing, his beloved Martha to the cause. "Every letter brings me such an account of her health that it is with great pain that I stay here," he wrote John Page. To Edmund Pendleton, the president of the Virginia Convention, he wrote: "I am sorry the situation of my domestic affairs renders it indispensably necessary that I should solicit the substitution of some other person here."

It is clear that along with his desire to express "the American mind," Jefferson poured deep personal anguish into the Declaration. He showed the draft to Adams and Franklin.

"Their alterations," he said, "were two or three only and merely verbal." (In the second paragraph, "sacred and undeniable" were changed to "self-evident," probably at Franklin's suggestion.) Jefferson meticulously rewrote the whole draft, adding some 16 corrections of his own, and reported it to the committee. Then it was thrown into the lap of Congress.

Lee's resolution passed on July 2. As far as Adams was concerned that was the historic day. "The 2nd day of July 1776," he wrote jubilantly, "will be the most memorable epocha in the history of America....It ought to be solemnized with pomp and parade, with shows, games, sports, guns, bells, bonfires, and illuminations from one end of the continent to the other, from this time forward, forevermore."

The fact of independence was accomplished. Now it was time to take up the declaration that would justify it to the world. The sharp-witted lawyers fell upon Jefferson's creation with a zeal that cut the sensitive author to the quick. For three days they slashed away at his paper, slicing off offensive words and phrases as if they were cancerous tissue.

Out of the more than 1,800 words, the Congress expunged 460, about one-fourth, including a famous passage accusing the king of waging "cruel war against human nature" by abetting the slave trade to the colonies.

Jefferson agonized through the ordeal. For propriety's sake he sat still and silent, "a passive auditor," he said, suffering more than his dignity would allow him to show. The burden of defense fell on Adams, who jumped up repeatedly, "fighting fearlessly for every word" as Jefferson testified later, forging a debt of friendship the author never forgot.

At one point Ben Franklin tried to salve Jefferson's hurt with an anecdote about a hat maker who had made a sign for his shop that said, "John Thompson, hatter, makes and sells hats for ready money," with a picture of a hat underneath.

Thompson showed the sign to friends, each of whom criticized some word or phrase. ("Sells hats!" cried one. "Why nobody expects you to give them away!") Thompson ended up with a picture of a hat and his name.

Finally on the evening of July 4 the slashing ceased. John Hancock, who presided over the proceedings, called for a vote. Twelve colonies voted yes; New York, which had not yet received instructions, abstained. When New York's instructions arrived on July 15 the vote became unanimous.

President Hancock ordered a public reading of the Declaration on July 8. Hundreds of townspeople embraced and cheered in the State House yard while Col. John Nixon, a local tavern keeper, read Jefferson's words from the balcony of an observatory tower.

But of all the patriots celebrating the Declaration, Jefferson was probably the least able to enjoy it. Not only had the Congress destroyed his pride of authorship, but the letters from home stopped coming again. "I wish I could be better satisfied on the point of Patty's recovery," he wrote Francis Eppes on July 15. "I have not heard from her at all for two posts before, and no letter from herself now."

His anxiety wasn't helped by Virginia's thinning ranks in the Congress. Debate had turned to the Articles of Confederation, and one by one the Virginia delegates were inventing excuses to go home. Almost before he knew it,

Jefferson was left as the sole guardian of Virginia's vote. On July 29 he issued a plea to Richard Henry Lee, who was supposed to replace him: "For God's sake, for your country's sake, and for my sake, come."

By September 3 Jefferson could stand it no longer. Even though Lee had not yet arrived, he set out for Monticello. En route he picked up his ailing wife and daughter at The Forest, and for a few precious weeks they enjoyed the autumn serenity of their mountaintop.

FOR YEARS JEFFERSON'S authorship of the Declaration of Independence remained an obscure fact of history known only to a few close friends and his colleagues in the Congress. Astonishingly, it was never publicly acknowledged until a Boston newspaper mentioned it in 1794. As late as 1800 Jefferson himself ranked it second in his own list of public accomplishments. At the top: clearing the Rivanna River near his home for shipping tobacco.

If Jefferson's preoccupations were mostly domestic, they continued to be dominated by Martha's health. In the first six years after he returned from Philadelphia she bore him four more children, but only two survived infancy. On May 3, 1782, the last was born. The child thrived, but the mother failed to recover. For four months Jefferson nursed her with desperate tenderness.

One day toward the end Martha opened the pages of *Tristram Shandy*, a popular novel of the period, and copied the following lines:

> *Time wastes too fast; every letter I trace tells me with what rapidity life follows my pen. The days and hours of it are flying over our heads like clouds of windy day never to return – more everything passes on –*

That was as far as her strength could take her. In a clear, firm hand her husband completed the quotation:

– and every time I kiss thy hand to bid adieu, every absence which follows it is prelude to that eternal separation which we are shortly to make!

On September 6, 1782, Jefferson recorded the saddest of all the items in his incredible account book: "My dear wife died this day at 11:45 a.m."

To assuage his grief, he plunged back into the political life he once vowed to avoid. During the next 26 years he was to serve as a Member of Congress, Minister to France, Secretary of State, Vice President, and President for two terms. He never remarried. Of his six children, only Martha survived him. Another daughter, Mary, died in 1804 at the age of 25, two months after her father was renominated for President.

IT'S A SAD IRONY of history that when Jefferson should have been celebrating two of the greatest events of his public life – the Declaration of Independence and his landslide re-election to the Presidency – he was privately tormented by anxiety and grief over two of the people closest to him.

Jefferson himself may have wondered whether his public service was worth the personal price. Had he been home the summer of 1776 when his wife most needed him, had he not exposed her to the rigors of the Revolutionary War that afterward attended his term as governor of Virginia, would she have lived beyond her 33 years? Indeed, if she had, would Jefferson, whose fondest wish in life was to enjoy domestic tranquility at Monticello with his wife and daughters and scientific pursuits, have become President?

Whatever the answers, Jefferson's last great wish – to live to the 50th anniversary of the Declaration of Independence – bears testimony to the significance he and the rest of the world came to attach to that document. Two days before his death he handed his daughter a poem that read in part:

Farewell, my dear, my lov'd daughter, adieu!
The last pang of life is in parting from you.

Two seraphs await me long shrouded in death;
I will bring them your love on my last parting breath.

Jefferson slept through the night. When he awoke he remarked, "This is the 4th of July." It was only the third. He fought with every ounce of his ebbing energy to live to the great day.

Finally at 50 minutes past noon, on July 4, 1826, he died—50 years to the day after the Declaration of Independence.

Five hundred miles to the north, in Quincy, Massachusetts, his old friend, sometime enemy, and compatriot in the Continental Congress, John Adams, was also dying. Of all the delegates back in 1776 he had fought the hardest for independence. He too wanted to see the great day.

When Adams said his last words early that evening, he didn't know that his friend had died just hours before. But now his words had another meaning.

"Thomas Jefferson," he said, "survives."

Originally published in the *Chicago Tribune Magazine,*" July 2, 1978.

James Michener

King of the Blockbusters

CORAL GABLES, Florida – Like those rambling, 900-page sagas that have made him America's top-selling novelist, James Michener just keeps going.

At 81, he's been grinding out big books longer than McDonald's has Big Macs, blending fact and fantasy into gigantic word feasts for an ever-devouring public.

The 36 books of James Albert Michener have been translated into 52 languages, nine movies, four television shows, and one musical, "South Pacific." His novels, such as *Chesapeake*, *Centennial*, *Poland* and *Texas*, generally hit the top of the best-seller list within a week of their official publication. His latest, *Alaska*, published last summer, had the biggest first-run printing ever (800,000 copies) of a hard-cover. He has, among his many awards, a Pulitzer Prize and the Presidential Medal of Freedom – the highest honor the nation bestows.

All the hoopla seems out of character for this quiet, sedate man who likes to say of his work: "Whatever I did, there was always someone around who was better qualified. They just didn't bother to do it." Yet five minutes after playing down his accomplishments, he is apt to boast: "Every one of my books is still in hard cover. The sales just go on and on."

Now, at a rented home here near the University of Miami, he's grinding out another blockbuster, a novel about

James Michener received the Presidential Medal of Freedom, the nation's highest civilian honor, from President Gerald Ford in 1977.

the Caribbean, which he says will be "the last of the big books."

If he keeps his word, it will be sayonara to a novel-writing career that has spanned two generations and spawned, by one estimate, some 60 million copies if you count the paperbacks.

Along the way he's seen more of the world than 10 other people combined. Wherever he researches a book, he digs in for a two- or three-year stint. He estimates that he's been to Singapore 50 times, Burma 20 times, and Bora Bora 8 times.

Almost three years have passed since he had quintuple-bypass surgery (23 years ago he suffered a near fatal heart attack). Yet under his khaki open-collar shirt and brown Bermuda shorts his frame is still spare, almost gaunt. His blue eyes, behind the bifocals, crackle with likely intelligence.

An old Royal typewriter presides at a corner of his sparsely furnished study. The most prominent collection of books is not his own but 30 volumes of the *Encyclopedia Britannica*—within easy reach like the tape deck behind his desk. Before we begin the interview, he turns off a Stravinsky opera.

"Music is really part of my life," he says. "Someday I want to write an opera book. I've been asked to, but I never seem to find the time."

Offering orange juice to their visitor, Mari Michener announces that she has to run some errands and tells her husband to have lunch at Rudolph's Barbecue. She's as spirited and forthright as her husband is withdrawn. She cites the names of some literary critics and warns: "My husband never reads reviews, but I read them all. And nobody better say anything bad about my husband."

Michener describes how he met Mari Yoriko Sabusawa, his wife of 33 years, at a luncheon in Chicago. The American-born daughter of Japanese parents, she was thrown into an internment camp after Pearl Harbor. Later she went to work as an editor for the American Library Association. She was 34, he was 47 and twice divorced. He was writing a story for

Life magazine on interracial marriage. She began the conversation by criticizing his latest novel, *Sayonara,* about a tragic romance between an American serviceman and his Japanese wife. "An interracial marriage doesn't have to end in tragedy," she said. A year later they decided to give it a try.

"Did you know the last song Irving Berlin wrote was the title song for the movie *Sayonara*? Michener says. "They've been trying to make a musical out of it for years."

Whether *Sayonara* ever makes it to Broadway, Michener goes on writing as if his life depends on it. "I live with the public," he says, "since I'm a complete freelance. I have no affiliations. Most of us can't make that, but those who do take it very seriously. We're totally aware that we're children of public fancy."

BY ANY STANDARD, Michener the freelance has had an amazingly adventurous life. By the time he was 19, he had hitchhiked through 45 states. Stationed on the island of Espiritu Santo during World War II, he began writing travel sketches while traveling around the Pacific. They became *Tales of the South Pacific,* which won the 1948 Pulitzer Prize and inspired the hit Broadway musical. (Michener once advised struggling writers on the key to success: "Make sure Rogers and Hammerstein read your first book.")

Michener's odyssey began in true Dickensian fashion. A foundling who never knew his natural parents, he was taken in at age 2 by Mabel Michener, a remarkable Quaker woman in Doylestown, Pa., who reared her son alongside many foster children who came and went. More than once, reduced circumstances forced her to send them to the local poorhouse. Not until he was 19 did he learn from an acquaintance that he was adopted.

The poverty of those early years still evokes an emotional response: "I never had skates, I never had a bicycle, I never had a wagon—nothing the other kids had. Nothing. A guy said he could never figure out how I tied my shoelaces because they were all just knots."

Despite their circumstances, Michener's mother made life at home a dazzling introduction to great books (he cites Milton, Dickens, Keats, Wordsworth and the Bible as his chief literary influences). It also brought him the solace of music. When Mable's brother bought the struggling family a Victrola, young Jim listened to Caruso in mesmerized silence.

"I learned from my mother," Michener says, "that there's a world into which even the most abjectly poor can pass freely. It saved me."

Michener's world soon reached out beyond Doylestown. "At 14 I left home with 35 cents in my pocket and hitched to Florida. It never occurred to me that I wouldn't make it. I think that before I was 15, I had been from Canada to Key West. Things on the road were just about as good as things at home. I think I traveled because I had an innate love of seeing what was around the bend. I've never lost that sense of curiosity."

After high school, he got a scholarship to Swarthmore College, from which he graduated *summa cum laude*. Later he became a social studies teacher and eventually a textbook editor at Macmillan.

"Education was the only way out for me," he said. "Learning was far more than just grades. It was a weapon in my hands. I mean, American universities were just made for me. If I had been born a Yugoslavian, I'd be counting gasoline drums."

Still, the poverty of Michener's childhood didn't stop there. He recalls the Depression years: "They have a deeper impact on someone like me than people realize. It makes you more dour, more tightly grained. It inhibits you. If you don't turn it to anger, which I never did, you're always aware that it could come back. I live as if I had stayed at my job and retired on a small pension and some savings and security, because I need to know what it's like."

Traces of those early years still permeate the Micheners' daily lives. Throughout their years of world travel, they have been based in an unpretentious home in Pipersville,

Pennsylvania. The home they stay in now is rented: a modest three-bedroom Spanish-style villa a few blocks from the University of Miami, where he holds the title "professor emeritus." ("What that means, nobody knows, but they've given me a secretary and the use of an office.")

There is little artwork on the walls, yet he and his wife gave the University of Texas (which hosted him when he wrote his novel about that state) a collection of 20th Century American art valued at several million dollars. A collection of 6,000 Japanese prints went to the Honolulu Academy of Art. They also have given away lavish chunks of their fortune to help struggling writers. They recently donated $2 million to Swarthmore and endowed a $500,000 scholarship fund for the Writers' Workshop at the University of Iowa.

That's a long way from Doylestown. Yet Michener's life epitomizes the stuff his novels are made of: common sense, frugality, hard work and good old-fashioned American virtue.

Like most of his novels, the one about the Caribbean will be drawn from intense on-the-scene research, hundreds of interviews with locals and just plain hanging out. It will have romance, adventure and history. And there will be good guys and bad guys (both real and imagined) to tie it all together. It's a formula millions love.

When industry insiders try to account for Michener's popularity, they talk about how his writing appeals to readers who don't normally read fiction.

Explains Albert Erskine, his long-time editor at Random House: "Jim isn't simply writing entertainment. People feel they learn a lot from him. He has the ability to anticipate developments in different parts of the world long before they happen. *Hawaii* came out just before statehood; *The Source*, when important events were taking place in Israel. As for *The Covenant*, you can't pick up the newspaper without finding stories about South Africa."

Michener downplays his sense of timing. "You don't have to be too bright to see that Poland had to come back into significance. Same about South Africa, Hawaii, the Middle

East, Japan—they were inevitable. Afghanistan. I saw it as clearly as if it had been drafted. It had to happen. And in my case it's usually been long in advance. Not because I'm a bright guy. I'm not. I'm a good solid Germanic type of character."

Owen Laster, Michener's literary agent at William Morris, suggests: "He's popular because he tells a wonderful story. You've sensed you learned something—information of a large nature. The families in his novels constantly connect, and the reader feels absorbed in his characters and expanded after reading one of his books."

Michener expresses bewilderment about his own wide appeal. "I think it's remarkable that a man could write the kind of thing I do—lengthy, intricate, not dependent on sex or violence—and acquire the kind of readership I have.

"I don't think the way I write books is the best or even the second best. The really great writers are people like Emily Bronte, who sit in a room and write out of their limited experience and unlimited imagination. I'm not a stylist like John Updike or Saul Bellow and I don't aspire to be. But I work very diligently to get a narrative flow. I'll sacrifice anything for that."

While other best-selling novelists often seem to take dead aim at the marketplace—what the public wants—Michener claims he writes about the things that interest him.

"I write pretty much for myself," he says. "The curious thing about my track record is that I've been able to write very freely about a wide scatter of subject matter and keep the public with me."

This much is certain: People read a Michener novel because he's the author. Following his usual pattern, he consulted dozens of experts for his book on the Caribbean. He does all his own research and writing. He does get help from his long-time assistant, John Kings, 64, who checks out books and Michener's final draft before it goes to the publisher. A former editor at Reader's Digest, the English-born Kings signed on as Michener's "field adviser" and all-around organizer for *Centennial* in 1972 and has stayed on ever since.

"John really is my business manager," Michener says. "He arranges all the travel. He's also very good at finding books for me. I don't go to the library much anymore. I tell him what I need. Just this morning he and Theresa (Potter, his secretary) made a list of all the books on the Caribbean they brought me. It's now somewhere around 350. I don't read them all, but I read indexes with a skill that's frightening."

Michener writes every day from 7:30 a.m. to shortly after noon. "I sit right here at this typewriter," he says, demonstrating with two fingers. "When I'm done with my draft, John reads it. See, everything here in pencil is his. Then I give it to Theresa and she puts it on the word processor. Can't work without it these days."

Michener ignores the critics who complain that his novels are too long. Texas-born Hughes Rudd, writing in the *New York Times Book Review,* said Michener's 1,096-page novel about Rudd's home state "contains enough paper to cover several New England counties. (It's) so heavy you could leave it on a Lubbock, Tex., coffee table in a tornado and find it there when everything else was still in the air over Kansas City." *Newsweek*'s Jack Beatty warned would-be readers of *Chesapeake*: "My best advice is don't read it; my second best is don't drop it on your foot."

But when critics assault his style (novelist Gary Jennings dubbed *Alaska* "a monumental slab of a narrative"), he becomes testy. "Where are the books of the great stylists that were printed in the same year mine were?"

Such as?

"Oh, I'm not gonna 'such as.' They're long gone. They're not in reprints. They're not in constant sales. I'm probably the only author all of whose books are still in hard cover because the sales just go on and on. *Hawaii* is selling just as well now as it did three years after it was published. It's on something like the 35th printing."

Will his books be read 100 years from now?

"That's terribly problematic. When *Moby Dick* was written, one would have been very perceptive to say that 100 years from now it would be studied in all the universities. Like Longfellow, God, he must have looked down his nose at the author of *Moby Dick* – who the hell is this guy? Or even Hawthorne. But now who reads Longfellow? And everybody reads *Moby Dick*. So that's a very dicey ballgame."

Looking back, Michener has no regrets except for a few novels he didn't write: one on Mexico ("It's just disgraceful that I haven't done that one"); one on Leningrad ("That was knocked out for health reasons"), and one on the Muslim world, which he started but never finished.

"At one time I knew it better than any American writer, maybe any other American, in that I had lived in all the Muslim countries except Arabia. I had a great feeling for it. But I never got it done. By one thing or another it got interrupted."

No doubt the book would have fit Michener's central theme that resonates through all his work: that the world would be a better place if we all just understood one other a little better.

"We're in this together," he says. "The brotherhood of man is what the human race is all about."

His last big book nearly done, Michener sits in his Coral Gables study two days before setting off on a trip to Hawaii. His wife insists he needs the break.

And when they return, who knows, maybe he'll finally get around to writing that opera book.

This story was first published in the *Chicago Tribune*, December 27, 1988.

Emmett Till

An Unlikely Icon

MONEY, Mississippi—After an all-night train ride from Chicago, Emmett "Bobo" Till, age 14, arrived the third week in August 1955 in Money, Mississippi, a dusty crossroads consisting of a gas station, a few stores, and a cotton mill on the Tallahatchie River. At the town line stood a sign that proclaimed, "Money—a good place to raise a boy."

Among the town's black inhabitants was Bobo's great uncle, an old sharecropper and part-time preacher named Mose Wright, who'd offered the boy a place to stay while he spent the last two weeks of his summer vacation with his cousins.

A few days after his arrival, early in the evening of August 24, Bobo and his cousins pulled up in a '46 Ford outside Bryant's Grocery & Meat Market on the only road through town. The store, which sold provisions to black sharecroppers and their families, was owned by Roy and Carolyn Bryant, a white couple in their early twenties.

Roy had opened the store when he got out of the 84th Airborne Division a few years before. Carolyn, a two-time beauty queen with black hair and black eyes, had dropped out of high school to marry him. The couple had two young sons and lived in quarters in back of the store. To earn extra cash, Roy worked as a trucker with his half-brother, J. W. Milam, who a century before would have been a slavery

Mamie Till-Mobley took this photograph of her son Emmett on Christmas Day 1954. It was the last picture taken of him alive.

plantation's typical overseer—blustery, six feet two, 235 pounds, proud of the way he "handled" blacks. Twelve years older than Roy, he'd received two combat medals in the war.

Roy was on a trucking run to New Orleans with his half-brother while Carolyn worked the store and her sister-in-law, Juanita Milam, watched their kids in the living quarters. William Bradford Huie, writing for *Look* magazine, described what happened:

> *Bobo's party joined a dozen other young Negroes in front of the store. Bryant had built checkerboards there. Some were playing checkers, others were wrestling and "kiddin' about girls." Bobo bragged about his white girl.* He showed the boys *a picture of a white girl in his wallet; and to their jeers of disbelief, he boasted of his success with her.*
>
> *"You talkin' mighty big, Bo," one youth said. "There's a pretty little white woman in the store. Since you know how to handle white girls, let's see you go in and get a date with her."*
>
> *"You ain't chicken, are yuh, Bo?" another youth taunted him.*
>
> *Bo had to fire or fall back. He entered the store, alone, stopped at the candy case. Carolyn was behind the counter, Bobo in front. He asked for two cents worth of bubble gum. She handed it to him. He squeezed her hand and said, "How about a date, Baby?"*

Although what happened in the store after that is unclear, Carolyn stormed out and got a pistol from the car. Frightened, Bobo's friends rushed him away, but not before Bobo—in one more attempt to demonstrate his bravado—whistled at her on his way out the door. Carolyn returned to the back of the store and told her sister-in-law what had happened. They agreed not to tell their husbands.

When Roy returned from his trucking run, a bystander told him what "the talk was" and about the black boy from Chicago who was staying at Preacher Wright's place. "Once Roy Bryant knew," wrote Huie the *Look* reporter, "...in the opinion of most white people around him, for him to have done nothing would have marked him as a coward and a fool."

Early in the morning of August 28, under the cover of darkness, Roy and his half-brother, J. W. Milam, showed up at Preacher Wright's house where his great nephew was staying and took him away in a pickup truck.

Three days later, on August 31, a fisherman saw a pair of feet sticking up from the Tallahatchie River. He notified the sheriff. A few hours later a decomposed corpse was pulled from the river, a cotton gin attached to the neck with barbed wire. The face was mutilated beyond recognition.

Preacher Wright, who had reported the kidnapping of his great nephew, was summoned to the scene. An undertaker preparing to take the body away turned to Mose and said, "I just removed this ring. Do you recognize it?"

Mose turned the ring over in his hand. Inscribed on it were the initials "L.T."

THE MURDER OF EMMETT TILL made national headlines. As details of the murder and its aftermath unfolded, so did the media coverage. Headlines in the *Chicago Sun-Times* and *Chicago Tribune* screamed, "SUSPECTS ENTER NOT GUILTY PLEA"..."TWO GO ON TRIAL FOR TILL MURDER"... "JURORS HEAR OF CONFESSION IN TILL TRIAL."

When Emmett's body arrived back in Chicago, Mamie Till Bradley went to the funeral home to claim it. Medgar Evers, the Mississippi field director of the NAACP, had warned her about what she would see when the undertaker opened the coffin.

"Can I make a suggestion?" he said.

Emmett's mother responded faintly. "What?"

Evers hesitated and drew in his breath. "I think you should have an open casket at your son's funeral."

"Why?"

"So the world will know what the white people in Mississippi did to your son."

It didn't matter that the brash teenager from Chicago had overstepped his bounds. In spite of his mother's warning about respecting white folks in Mississippi and addressing them as "Sir" and "Ma'am," he had violated an unwritten law of the Jim Crow South: He had flirted with a white woman—an act that cost him his life. All over the country, people wondered whether his punishment fit the crime.

On Saturday, September 3, 1955—three days after Emmett Till's body was pulled out of the Tallahatchie River—thousands of people filed past his open casket at Robert's Temple of the Church of God in Christ on Chicago's South Side. *Jet* magazine ran photos of the mutilated corpse. In Charleston, Mississippi, H.C. Strider, the Tallahatchie County sheriff who had presided over the recovery at the river, told reporters he didn't think the body was Till's. "The whole thing," he scoffed, "looks like a deal made up by the National Association for the Advancement of Colored People."

Just the same, Roy Bryant, 24, the grocer from Money, and his half-brother, J.W. Milam, 36, were in custody on murder and kidnapping charges. Circuit Court Judge Curtis Swango set their trial for September 19 at the Tallahatchie County court house in Sumner. In Mississippi the maximum sentence for murder was death; for kidnapping, ten years. But nobody in Tallahatchie County expected a white defendant—let alone two white defendants—to be found guilty of the murder of a black person. It had never happened in the 160-year history of Mississippi, and if the white folks had their way it wasn't going to happen this time either.

THE *CHICAGO TRIBUNE* sent a reporter named Paul Holmes down to Mississippi to cover the trial. On Monday morning, September 19, the day the trial was to begin, Holmes's first dispatch appeared on page 1:

Sumner, Miss.—Here in a rich cotton country of the Mississippi delta region, where not one of the county's 19,000 Negroes is registered to vote, two white men charged with the murder of a Chicago Negro boy will go on trial before an all-male, all-white jury.

This is Tallahatchie County, a sunny fertile flatland, cut into two judicial districts by the deep, swift flowing Tallahatchie River, where cotton fields stretch from horizon to horizon and opulent planters live a gracious, luxurious life in their feudal baronies.

Strict segregation of Negroes and whites is the rule here. There are separate schools, separate drinking fountains, separate washrooms, and separate restaurants. Segregation is the cornerstone of this region's society and economy....

The two white men who will go on trial are in effect pawns in a wider, deeper game than a mere murder trial. They are frankly regarded as symbols of the delta region's tenacious grasp on things as they are. Their fate, and reactions from the country to that fate, are expected to be a trial balloon in the region's resistance to social change.

Back in Chicago, kids Emmett's age—black and white both—were paying special attention. Mr. Rubedo, a ninth grade civics teacher, laid the *Tribune* down on his desk. "Anybody want to take bets on what's going to happen?"

One kid replied evasively, "The jury will decide that."

"Okay, you pass Civics 101."

For Mr. Rubedo's students, the trial in Sumner, Mississippi, would be a civics lesson, designed to show how things are supposed to work in a structured society. But it would also show how things work when put to the test of human nature.

IN THEIR SECOND FLOOR CELL at the Tallahatchie County Jail, Roy Bryant and J. W. Milam complained they were losing good money while awaiting their trial. The cotton harvest was in full swing and the sharecroppers had extra cash to spend. Of the trial's outcome they had no doubt. A sampling of public opinion had produced not one white person in Tallahatchie County who expected a guilty verdict. Moreover, all five lawyers who comprised the active bar of Sumner, the county seat, had stepped forward to represent the defendants *pro bono.* Their plan was to dispute the identity of the body found in the Tallahatchie River. If successful—and they had no reason to believe they would fail—they would ask Judge Swango for a directed verdict of not guilty.

As for the ring Emmett Till's mother had given him—the one inscribed with his father's initials—the defense answer to that would be that Till had never worn it in Mississippi. How could the prosecution prove otherwise? It would be Preacher Wright's word against the sheriff's.

TWELVE WHITE JURORS—an insurance agent, two carpenters, and nine farmers—had been selected and sequestered in Sumner's only hotel, the Delta Inn, across the railroad tracks from the red brick courthouse. Each had given his word that he had no racial prejudice, that he could sit in fair and impartial judgment on the two white men accused of killing a Negro. Reporters, photographers, and TV cameramen fanned out across the courthouse square seeking out locals for comments. Thus the town, which numbered about 550 souls, braced for the biggest week in its history.

When the trial got underway, the defendants and their families showed up in their Sunday best. Roy Bryant and J. W. Milam and their wives became instant celebrities. Reporters buzzed about the Bryants' handsome looks. One likened Carolyn Bryant, the two-time beauty queen, to Marilyn Monroe.

Whites from all over the region jammed into the courtroom to witness the spectacle. Many brought picnic baskets and ice cream. Some brought their children. A handful of blacks looked on from a segregated section in the back. Sheriff H.C Strider, behind an unlit cigar, watched from the side, his three-hundred-pound frame giving sufficient warning to any would-be trouble-maker,

The prosecution called Mose "Preacher" Wright to the stand. The old sharecropper described how the two men showed up at his house the night before his great nephew,

Emmett "Bobo" Till, was abducted. The house, a wooden shack with a screened-in porch, sat fifty feet off a gravel road. Preacher heard a knock on the door at 2:30 in the morning and called out, "Who's that?"

"Mr. Bryant from Money."

Preacher got up and went out to the porch.

"You got a boy from Chicago here?" Bryant asked.

"Yessir.

"I want to talk to him."

Preacher led Bryant and the other man to a back room where Bobo and three of his cousins were sleeping. Bryant told the preacher to turn on the light. It didn't work. The other man, taller than Bryant and with a bald head, held a flashlight in one hand, a pistol in the other. He pointed the flashlight at Bobo's face and said, "You the nigger who did the talking?"

"Yeah," Bobo replied, half awake.

"Don't 'yeah' me, boy. I'll blow your head off. Get your clothes on."

Preacher continued his testimony. "I told them he was my nephew, a stranger here in town and didn't know what he was doing. I said, 'Please don't take him.' My wife even offered to pay them. The man with the flashlight said, 'You niggers go back to sleep.' Then they took the boy."

When the prosecutor asked him to identify the men who came into his house, Preacher stood up and pointed his finger at the two defendants – Roy Bryant and J.W. Milam.

A tense silence fell over the courtroom. It was the first time in Mississippi that a black man had accused a white man of murder before a judge and jury. To make such an accusation was to invite the revenge of a potential lynch mob. Unwilling to take any chances, Medgar Evers, the man from the NAACP, waited outside the courtroom prepared to whisk the old sharecropper to safety.

Preacher's testimony wasn't finished.

"I hand you a ring," the prosecutor said, "and I ask you to tell the court and jury if that is the ring the undertaker took off Emmett's finger."

Preacher looked at the ring with Emmett's father's initials. "Yessir, it is."

"How do you know?" a defense attorney asked the Preacher on cross-examination. Not satisfied with his response, the defense attorney asked the judge for a ruling on the testimony just given.

Turning to the jury box, Judge Swango said, "You gentlemen will disregard the statement that he (Preacher Wright) knew it was Emmett's ring."

Chief defense attorney John Whitten had no need to put his clients on the stand. The arresting officers testified that Roy Bryant and J.W. Milam said the boy they picked up at Preacher Wright's place "wasn't the right one," and so they let him go. In any event, the defendants were on trial for murder, not kidnapping.

Sheriff H.C. Strider testified that the body found at the river wasn't the right one either. "All I could tell, it was a human being," he said. Two expert witnesses claimed the victim had been dead eight to ten days, much longer than Emmett Till would have been dead when the body was recovered.

Whitten, the defense attorney, rose to make his closing argument. "Every last Anglo-Saxon one of you men in this jury," he said, "has the courage to set these men free."

At 2:34 p.m. on Friday, September 23, Judge Swango sent the jury out for deliberation. At 3:42 p.m., the announcement came that the jury had reached a verdict. The spectators stiffened. Reporters' notebooks were raised and cameras were poised to covey the announcement to the world.

SIX HUNDRED AND FIFTY MILES to the north, on Saturday, September 24, a banner headline jumped out from the *Chicago Tribune*: "ACQUIT TWO IN TILL SLAYING."

Sumner, Miss. (Sept. 23) – Two local white men accused of slaying a Chicago Negro were found not guilty today by an all-white, all-male jury. The foreman said the jurors refused to believe that a body fished from a river Aug. 28 was that of the supposed victim, Emmett Till, 14.

The paper showed the Bryants and Milams celebrating with a smile and an embrace. The article described how relatives and friends crowded around them shaking hands and murmuring their approval of the verdict.

The jurors received slaps on the back and compliments like "good work" and "nice going." It had taken them one hour and eight minutes to reach a verdict. One of the jurors said it wouldn't have taken so long if they hadn't stopped to drink pop.

The verdict created an international firestorm. News articles and editorials across the country and in Europe condemned the verdict—and the State of Mississippi. Mamie Till Bradley, the NAACPs Medgar Evers, and other black leaders hoped Bryant and Milam would at least be punished for kidnapping.

Three weeks before the grand jury met to consider the kidnapping charge, Mississippi Senator James Eastland was in the news with information he'd dug up on Emmett Till's father. Private Louis Till, assigned to the 177th Port Company, 397th Port Battalion in Italy during the war, had been executed July 2, 1945, by the U.S. Army for the rape of two women and the murder of another. The implication was that bad blood ran in the family.

After the disclosure about her deceased husband, Mamie Till Bradley wondered how a senator, not a widow, could obtain that information. The grand jury refused to indict Roy Bryant and J.W. Milam for kidnapping. FBI Director J. Edgar Hoover declared to the press: "There has been no allegation made that the victim (Emmett Till) has been subjected to the deprivation of any right or privilege which is secured and protected by the Constitution and the laws of the United States."

Thousands of letters protesting the murder verdict poured into the White House. Mamie took her fight to the people and gave speeches to overflowing crowds across the country. Blacks were galvanized. Membership in the NAACP soared. Those in the trenches of the fledging civil rights movement knew they had to move boldly or lose their momentum.

On Thursday, December 1, 1955, Rosa Parks, a quiet department store seamstress, refused to give up her seat to a white passenger on a city bus in Montgomery, Alabama. Police arrested her for violating a municipal segregation ordinance, and a judge fined her $14.

On Saturday, December 3, 1955, Martin Luther King, Jr., a twenty-six-year-old black preacher at Montgomery's Dexter Avenue Baptist Church, called for a city-wide bus boycott. Five thousand black residents responded and many more would follow.

One hundred days after Emmett Till's body was pulled from the Tallahatchie River, the American civil rights movement was born.

Distributed by TransAmerica Syndicate, Inc., August 28, 2010. For a recent development in the Emmett Till case, Google "Carolyn Bryant Donham, *Boston Globe*, July 14, 2022." Donham died April 25, 2023.

Tova, Frieda & Rachel

Hitler's Youngest Survivors

OSWIECIM, POLAND – About a mile outside this little industrial town in southern Poland lay the remains of Auschwitz-Birkenau, the Nazi concentration camp where up to 1.5 million people were murdered during World War II.

As the Soviet army advanced westward in the closing months of the war, the Nazis evacuated 60,000 prisoners from the camp, sending them off on a death march to Germany.

On January 27, 1945, the first Soviet regiment arrived at the gate, disconnected the electrified wires, and freed the camp's 7,000 remaining prisoners, many of them near death from exposure and starvation.

Among the youngest survivors were three Jewish girls from Tomaszow Mazowiecki, a town in central Poland. The oldest was 10, the youngest was 6. Each bears witness to the horrors of the camp and the joy of their liberation.

"Nothing that happened in this universe compares to what happened at Auschwitz during the war," declared Tova Friedman, now 66, a resident of Highland Park, N.J.

"My mother once told me that I was the youngest person to survive Auschwitz," Tova said. "I don't know that for a fact, but I never saw anyone younger or smaller there, and I was pretty small for a 6-year-old."

Still, Tova has vivid memories of her eight-month stay, because her mother, who also survived Auschwitz, told her stories about it later that etched the images of horror in her mind.

"I once calculated the odds of all three members of my family - my mother, my father, and myself - surviving the war as Polish Jews," Tova said. "It came to one in one thousand. We were among the lucky ones."

Tova's once blond hair, now reddish brown with streaks of gray, frames her round expressive face. Her eyes crackle with lively intelligence, but there's a haunting sadness behind them.

"I suffer when I think about the 6 million Jews who

Young prisoners from the Kinderlager including six-year-old Tova Friedman (left) show their tattoos to their Soviet liberators.

didn't make it," she said.

Indeed, Tova suffers when she thinks about her Polish homeland, where nine out of 10 Jews perished during Hitler's reign of terror. And she suffers when she thinks about her four grandparents and her mother's nine brothers and sisters who died, most of them in Nazi camps.

Yet, through a series of good fortune, she and her parents survived, as did two friends she made in the Tomaszow ghetto in the early days of the war.

Her friends weren't as lucky. Rachel Hyams lost her father in a cattle car destined for Auschwitz. Tova's other friend from Tomaszow, Frieda Tenenbaum, now 70 and living in Cambridge, Mass., lost her 4-year-old sister in a labor camp. Rachel and Frieda were 7 and 10 when the Russians freed them from Auschwitz.

All three were prisoners in the *Kinderlager* – the "children's camp" – a section of Auschwitz that housed 20,000 Gypsy inmates before the Nazis sent them to their deaths in July 1944.

Frieda, the oldest, recalls the day they were freed:

"At sunrise we heard the distant boom of guns, then scattered shouts from around the camp. On the east horizon we saw hundreds of soldiers marching toward us in tattered uniforms. Some of them were holding up red flags."

At 1 o'clock in the afternoon the Russians arrived at the gate. Their leader, a Jewish colonel, entered the children's barracks.

"When he saw us he broke down and wept," Frieda said.

Tova's recollection of Liberation Day is reinforced by stories her mother told her after the war. "Suddenly my mother showed up at the Kinderlager. She was very agitated and said, 'They're sending us on a march.' She took my hand and we ran into a camp hospital where she laid me next to a corpse. Then she pulled a blanket over me and said, 'Don't move.'" Then came the Nazis' order to evacuate the camp: "*Alle Juden raus!* All Jews out!"

"There was lots of shooting and we smelled smoke,"

Tova said. "Finally, my mother, who was hiding a few feet away, said, 'The building is on fire. We've got to get out.' We saw SS guards in the distance marching people away and setting buildings on fire behind them.

"We stood by the barbed wires and waited," Tova said. "Mother told me not to touch them because I might be electrocuted. When the Russians arrived, they disconnected the wires and set up field stoves to feed us. Mother and I hugged each other and cried."

More and more people came out of hiding as word got out that Auschwitz was freed. Some prisoners had to be carried out of their barracks. Others lay on the ground in the last stage of starvation. Within a week about half the prisoners died. For them liberation came too late.

Frieda recalls being photographed with other children after their liberation. The film, shot by a Soviet crew, shows a group of children in striped uniforms marching between two rows of barbed wires. Frieda's mother is holding a child.

The liberators were already in a propaganda mode. "The children never had uniforms at Auschwitz," Frieda said. "But the Russians wanted to show the world that they were freeing little prisoners from the Germans, so they had us put them on."

Between 1.1 million and 1.5 million people were murdered at Auschwitz between 1940 and 1945, making it the deadliest of the Nazi camps. Although the exact numbers will never be known, it is believed that a million of the victims were Jews.

Tova and Rachel arrived at Auschwitz in June 1944 after a two-year stint with their parents at a slave labor camp. Frieda, who had gone to another labor camp with her parents and younger sister, arrived in July. Her sister was seized there in a children's selection. Years later Frieda learned she was trucked to a nearby woods and shot.

After their arrival at Auschwitz, the three girls from Tomaszow constantly faced the threat of death. Their closest call came when they were led to separate gas chambers, only to be sent back to their barracks. Frieda was spared after prisoners dynamited Crematorium IV - one of five crematoriums at Auschwitz - on October 7, 1944.

Tova and Rachel were spared at Crematorium II because of a clerical error. "I remember standing in the undressing room with an orange towel wrapped around me," Tova said. "The SS guard couldn't find our tattoo numbers on his clipboard, so he sent us back."

Tova's number was A27633. Rachel's was one ahead of hers, A27632. The two girls had stood in line together when they were tattooed at the Kinderlager. The blue markings on their left forearms still bear evidence of their ordeal.

But the ordeal didn't end with their liberation. "After the Russians freed us, we had no place to go," Tova said.

The war had wiped out virtually all the Jewish population of Tomaszow, and anti-Semitism was still rampant in Poland. What followed were a series of displaced persons (DP) camps in Germany and finally their immigration to North America.

Rachel, her mother, and stepfather - her mother remarried in the DP camp - moved to Montreal in January 1948. Tova and Frieda came to the United States in 1949 and 1950 after President Harry Truman lifted immigration restrictions against Jewish refugees.

In the summer of 2004, sixty years after entering Auschwitz as children, two of the three survivors, Friedman and Tenenbaum, together with Friedman's daughter, Itaya Friedman of Bridgewater, N.J., and Tenenbaum's son, Abraham ("Bo") Grayzel of Portland, Ore., returned to Poland to film their story for a PBS special.*

"It was very difficult to go back and relive what happened, but it was something I felt I needed to do,"

*The 90-minute special, "Surviving Auschwitz: Children of the Shoah," first aired May 18, 2005, in commemoration of the 60th anniversary of the Allied victory in Europe. To view it online, Google "PBS Surviving Auschwitz."

Tenenbaum said.

The trip was a watershed experience.

"I feel strengthened and more open," she said afterward. "I find I am more able to allow myself to feel grief and feel the pain of grief."

Today, Auschwitz is a grim reminder of the Nazis' atrocities against Jews and other targets of the Third Reich: Poles, Gypsies, Russians, homosexuals, Jehovah's Witnesses.

It is actually a complex of three camps. The main camp, Auschwitz I, contains several rows of three-story brick buildings built during World War I to house Polish soldiers. At first glance it might appear to be a college campus; neatly trimmed poplar trees line the roads between the buildings.

But appearances deceive, just as the iron sign over the gate deceived the camp's inmates 75 years ago. The sign, still there, reads: "*Arbeit macht frei*" ("Work makes you free"). A hundred yards away a crematorium lies half hidden in the ground.

Construction of Auschwitz II (Birkenau) began in 1942 after Hitler put into effect his "Final Solution" - the extermination of the European Jews. The vast expanse of the camp boggles the imagination.

At the peak of its operation in 1944 Birkenau contained nearly two square miles of wooden barracks that housed more than 100,000 prisoners. Most of the barracks are gone; spindly brick chimneys mark the places were they once stood. At the end of the railroad track stands a monument flanked by broken slabs of concrete. These are the ruins of Birkenau's four gas chambers and crematoriums, left just as they were when the retreating Nazis blew them up. Each crematorium was capable of burning 5,000 bodies per day.

Auschwitz III (Monowice) was a synthetic rubber plant on the other side of town that employed slave labor for the German war effort. The factory, operated by I.G. Farben, is still in operation.

But it's the huge Birkenau camp that stands out from the others. "This is the largest graveyard in human history," declared Jerzy Wroblewski, director of the Auschwitz-Birkenau State Museum, which has maintained the site since 1947. For Jews it has become the symbol of the Holocaust.

Museum officials are planning a special ceremony to mark the 60th anniversary of the camp's liberation. Homage will be paid to the victims by Polish President Aleksander Kwasniewski and heads of state from around the world.

But for the three girls from Tomaszow, it will be a day of reflection. They will exchange 60th "birthday" cards and talk about what it means to be alive. "We think of January 27 as our spiritual birthday," Frieda said.

This story originally appeared in the *Chicago Tribune*, January 29, 2005.

Peter VandenBosch

The Last of the Greatest Generation

CERIGNOLA, Italy—On the fifth day of February 1945, Pete VandenBosch and his flight crew landed at the 15th Air Force Base in Cerignola, Italy. Situated on the back side of the boot near the Adriatic coast, Cerignola was a town of little note except it boasted of green olives and a family named LaGuardia whose favorite son, a boy named Fiorello, had grown up to become the mayor of New York City.

Like the town, the base didn't amount to much. It consisted of a temporary airstrip for launching bombing raids against the Germans. A makeshift control tower jutted out from a cluster of whitewashed buildings. A half dozen barracks housed the enlisted men.

Pete, a radio operator on a B-24, and his crew had just settled into their bunks when their commanding officer, Colonel Snowden, called them into his office.

"Gentlemen," he said, pointing to a map. "I need you to fly up to northern Austria and take out an installation there. You'll probably encounter enemy fire."

Pete's heart leapt to his throat. This would be his first combat mission, and the trip would be a long one—three hundred miles up the Adriatic, then over the Alps and all the way up to northern Austria to hit their target and back again.

Not only that, they would be flying over German anti-aircraft guns once they passed the 45th parallel.

Without a word, the crew returned to their barracks. Without looking at each other they put on their flight jackets and headed out to the runway.

They were about to board the plane when Billy Bruton said out of the blue, "Fellas, we gotta get down on our knees."

"Hearing a GI say that surprised me," Pete said. "Back in training, Bill told me he had been raised a Baptist, but we never talked religion after that. Now he was telling his buddies to get down and pray. It must have worked, because

World War II vet Peter VandenBosch, shown here in his twin-engine Beechcraft, founded Wings of Mercy, a non-profit air ambulance service, after he retired.

we returned from our mission without so much as getting shot at."

Their next mission was to bomb Brenner Pass, the German army's main access route in the Alps between Austria and Italy. As they approached their target, Pete spotted anti-aircraft guns pointing up at them from the mountains.

The bay doors opened, releasing a half-dozen 1,000-pound bombs. Pete watched them explode when they hit the rocks. A few seconds later, through his headphones, he heard Troy Shields, the tail gunner, shout: "Antiaircraft fire coming from behind!"

A clashing sound, like knives and forks dropping into a dishpan, hit the plane. Shrapnel. The plane jolted. The explosion's force pushed the plane up and flattened him to the floor. He struggled back to his feet and heard the captain's voice in his headphones: "Pete, you okay?"

"Okay," he answered.

"Tommy?"

"Okay."

"Bill?"

"Okay."

"Troy?"

No answer.

"Troy?"

Still no answer.

Pete's heart stopped. He scurried over to the turret and found Troy crumpled over, pale as a sheet but otherwise okay. The explosion's impact had disconnected his microphone.

So it went, more or less, for seven missions. Each time the Americans hit their target, and each time they thanked God for sparing them. But they knew they couldn't defy the odds forever. The law of averages would see to that.

May 7, 1945, EARLY AFTERNOON. A junior officer popped his head into the barracks and said, "Put on your dress uniforms, men. The colonel wants us to line up on the runway."

Pete and his buddies knew what was coming. After the Allies closed in from all sides—England from the north, the U.S. from the west and south, and the Russians from the east—the German forces were in a shambles.

After everyone at the base assembled on the runway, Colonel Snowden's voice came over the P.A. "I suspect this comes as no surprise," he said, "but today the Germans announced their surrender."

When the cheering died down, the colonel continued: "Our chaplain will lead us in a prayer of thanksgiving."

When the chaplain finished his prayer, he handed the microphone back to the colonel.

"And now," the colonel said," we're going to celebrate!"

Two B-24s circled overhead.

"See those planes," he said, pointing to the sky. "This morning I ordered them up with a load of beer. When they come down, each man can have two bottles and no more. Is that clear?

Since the base lacked refrigerators, there was no way to chill the beer but to send it up on the planes. At ten thousand feet the beer was thirty degrees cooler than it would have been on the ground. "When those planes came in," Pete said, "what a celebration we had! Who cared if it was two o'clock in the afternoon?"

While most of the pilots were lieutenants, Sandy was a captain because of his combat experience. By the time of the German surrender, he had become the colonel's personal assistant, and he took advantage of the perks. Rounding up the crew of his B-24 he said, "We're going on a little sightseeing trip."

Three hours later his plane was over Munich. Sandy banked the plane over the city so his crew could get a good look. Seventy-one Allied air raids over a six-year period had reduced it to a pile of rubble.

But the war wasn't over. The Japanese were still going at it, and the 15th Air Force was getting ready to redeploy to the Pacific. Pete had already packed his belongings and was ready to leave when an announcement came over the P.A. system: "VandenBosch report to headquarters immediately."

Colonel Snowden looked at him from behind a stack of papers on his desk. "You've been assigned to the Mediterranean Air Transport Command," he said. "An aircraft will be here tomorrow to pick you up."

Pete's heart sank.

He returned to the barracks where his buddies were waiting - Troy, Bill, all the others. "For six months I had been living with these guys, eating with them, flying with them," Pete said later. "We were like brothers, and now I had to deliver this bombshell.

"I'm being redeployed," Pete told his buddies. "Mediterranean ATC. I'm leaving first thing tomorrow for Naples. Just like that I was gone."

In Naples Pete learned terrestrial navigation and joined a new squadron. His plane was a C-87, a transport version of the B-24. Every day he would fly generals, medical supplies, personnel and equipment to cities all over Europe and the Middle East - Berlin, Vienna, Athens, Cairo, Alexandria, Benghazi. "In the space of two months I saw more of the world than I ever did before," he said.

Then came another redeployment order. "That was how the Air Corps worked," he said. "You got your notice, you packed, and off you went. No discussion." This time he was going to the Pacific on a supply ship.

Pete waited with his squadron at the deployment center while the ship was being loaded. With nothing else to do, he and his new buddy Ray Robinson went to see a concert the Andrews Sisters were putting on for the GIs. The auditorium was so full that guys were perched on rafters.

Despite the Andrews Sisters' attempt to lift the GI's spirits, the mood was dour because most of them were being shipped to the Pacific. One of the sisters, Patty, had just finished a number when the commanding officer came out on stage, tapped her on the shoulder, and whispered into her ear. Patty handed him the microphone.

The commanding officer held the microphone to his mouth, drew in his breath, and said, "Japan has surrendered. The war is over."

"You could have heard a pin drop," Pete said.

"I repeat," the commander said, "the war is over. You don't have to go to the Pacific!"

At that instant pandemonium broke loose. "Everyone in the auditorium hooted and hollered," Pete recalled. "Ray and I broke down and cried."

On stage, Patty was crying too. "It's over! It's over!" she kept saying, unaware that her microphone was still open.

A pair of fatigues dropped down from the rafters, followed by the GI who had worn them. He didn't care if he got hurt. Neither did the guys he landed on. They had been through a lot worse in combat, and now they were going home.

"I hooted and hollered and cried with everybody else, because I was going home too," Pete said.

Or so he thought.

PETE HAD ALREADY MISSED going home once. While most of the GIs were heading across the Atlantic, he was still waiting for his ship to the Pacific - eight thousand miles in the opposite direction - and not feeling very good about it.

His buddy Ray Robinson was in the same boat, so to speak. They decided since they weren't going home that they would grant themselves a leave. As Pete saw it, the Air Corps owed it to them, and by golly they deserved it.

Rome seemed the logical place to go; it was a two-hour drive up the coast from Naples, and they had never seen it on the ground, only from the air on their ATC flights. The only problem was, they had no way to get there.

Knowing full well they wouldn't get permission if they asked for it, they commandeered a motorcycle from an army depot and disguised it with a number from their outfit. On the back they tied two canvas sacks with their clothes inside and a cardboard box. Then off they sped on their joy-ride with Pete at the controls and Ray holding on for dear life.

So what was in the box? Enough cigarettes to kill a platoon. Thanks to the tobacco lobby in Washington, every GI was issued one pack of cigarettes a day. Companies like Philip Morris and R.J. Reynolds knew what they were doing: What better way to hook a soldier for life than to give him free cigarettes for two years? It was a smart investment.

Their plan after they got to Rome was to sell the cigarettes on the black market. Some of the cigarettes they had saved from their rations. Most of them they had collected from guys in their outfit, buying them at fifty-five cents a carton or writing their names down so they could pay them on their return.

If you were to visit Rome today and needed a place to stay, your search might begin with Google or, if you waited until you arrived, a visit to the APT, the city's official tourist agency, which would direct you to a hotel. But in 1945 the place to begin—at least for GIs on the town—was the Red Cross, which matched you up with a host family.

Their host family turned out to be a thirty-something-year old man and his wife and three children. They all spoke fluent English. When the two GIs arrived at their apartment, the man asked what they had in the box.

"Cigarettes," Pete said.

"Are you smoking them?"

"No, we're selling them." Pete didn't mention their plan to sell them on the black market; it was something people assumed.

"How much?"

"Twelve dollars a carton."

"How many cartons do you have?"

"Twenty. That's how many we have in the box."

"I'll give you $200 for the whole box," he said.

"Sold," Pete said, and they made the exchange.

Over the next five days the host and his wife showed their American guests the sights of Rome - the Colosseum, the Roman Forum, Trevi Fountain, the Pantheon, the Vatican. "They treated us like old friends," Pete said. "When it was time to leave, I felt guilty about charging the man $200 for the cigarettes and offered to refund his money.

"Oh no, you keep it," he said.

"But I took advantage...."

"No, no, no," he interrupted. "It's a small price to pay to have our freedom back. If you - the Americans - hadn't come, who knows what would have happened to us under Hitler?"

"Or Mussolini," his wife added.

The two Americans exchanged hugs with their Italian friends and waved from their motorcycle as they sped away. Two hours later they quietly returned the stolen motorcycle to its place at the army depot.

NOW THAT THE WAR WAS OVER, the Army Air Corps' task in Italy was to mop up their operations of men and materials. They didn't seem to know what to do with Pete—at least as he saw it. Once again, the Air Corps deployed him to the ATC, this time to fly stretcher patients back to the United States. "Mostly we flew C-46's, big old twin-engine props we called whales; that's how most of the wounded GIs got home. All the while I kept wondering when my turn would come to go home."

In December his turn finally came. While the plane loaded up on the tarmac, Pete lay in his bunk listening to Fred Waring and the Pennsylvanians.

The plane was ready to take off. But at that moment a gust of wind off the Mediterranean blew another airplane into it, taking out the engine on the right wing. Once again, he was stuck.

Thanks to an intervention from the commanding officer (apparently, he never found out about the motorcycle), Pete and his buddy Ray secured two places on the *USS Monterey*, an aircraft carrier bound for Newport News, Virginia.

They boarded the ship three days before Christmas—December 22, 1945. After the horn sounded, the two stood on the deck and watched the dock slip away. Pete turned to Ray and said, "You know what's going to happen." It was a statement of fact more than a question.

"No, what's going to happen?"

"They're going to stop this ship at the Rock of Gilbraltar and they're going to announce over the P.A. system, 'Ray Robinson and Peter VandenBosch come forward,' and they're going to take us off this ship and send us back."

Ray laughed. "He obviously felt more confident about going home than I did," Pete said. "It wasn't until we got twenty miles out into the Atlantic—and out of sight of the Rock—that my jitters went away. The voyage was rough, but I didn't care. On Christmas Day I stood on the deck and let the ocean spray hit my face."

As the *USS Monterey* proceeded across the Atlantic, the waves grew higher. The ship, longer than two football fields, tossed back and forth like a teeter-totter. "One night a stream of vomit rained down from the bunk above me and splattered on the floor," Pete said.

Eventually the storm subsided. Pete craved a drink of milk. "I hadn't had a drink of milk in two years. It was something I had always taken for granted. It occurred to me that freedom was something I had always taken for granted, too, like drinking milk. If the war taught me anything, it's that freedom isn't handed to you like a glass of milk."

The ship arrived at Newport News on New Year's Eve, 1945. Pete and Ray watched from the deck as the first of the five thousand GIs onboard the ship filed down the gangplank. A brass band waiting on shore struck up "America the Beautiful." Finally, Pete and Ray made their way down the gangplank.

"When Ray got off the ship he knelt down and kissed the ground," Pete said. "When I got off the ship I knelt down and kissed the ground too."

Adapted from *Earth Angels: The Story of Peter VandenBosch and Wings of Mercy,* Deep River Books, 2011.

Part Three: Viewpoints

Hell

Divining Dante

TO: Satan@hell.com
FROM: DanteAlighieri@heaven.com
DATE: December 17, 1999 (earth time)

Dear Satan:

I can't believe how time flies up here. Do you realize it's been almost 700 years since Virgil, my guide, introduced me to you in Hell? It was Good Friday, 1300 A.D. to be exact.

After my trip to the Other Side, I thought about all the interesting people I met and put them into a poem, *The Divine Comedy*. Back on Earth they say it's the greatest poem ever written. But judging from the sales figures on Amazon.com, it looks like only a few lit majors read it anymore.

Anyway, since I have nothing to do up here but play the harp, I'm thinking of doing an update for 2000 A.D. Maybe it will boost sales. Problem is, I need a new cast of sinners from the 20th century. Since I've been out of human contact for a while, I thought you could help me out.

Yours,
Dante Alighieri

P.S. FYI, I'm attaching the first edition with all three parts—"Inferno," "Purgatorio" and "Paradiso," so you can see how they fit together.

Dante's not-so-funny *Divine Comedy* inspired Michelangelo's painting of this poor lost soul descending into hell.

REPLY TO: DanteAlighieri@heaven.com
FROM: Satan@hell.com
DATE: December 18, 1999

Dear Dante:

Glad to help, and thanks for attaching your first edition. I read just the "Inferno" part because that's the only one that interests me. You got it about right with the nine circles spiraling down to the pit of Hell. Each circle holds a different group of sinners; the lower the circle, the worse the punishment.

As for Circle 1 we have nobody new—still the same old blameless souls who lived before Christianity came along. Your friend Virgil is here. So are Socrates, Plato and Aristotle. They just sit in Limbo, staring off into space. But compared to the others, they have it pretty good.

In Circle 2 we have the gluttons buried in mountains of fat. Most of them are Americans; same with the hoarders and wasters in Circle 3. If fact, we have more Americans here than anyone else.

In Circles 4 and 5 we have the wrathful and sullen puffing and blowing smoke in each other's eyes. Even the surgeon general's warning doesn't stop them. Ever hear of Father Coughlin? Or George Wallace? Their rants against Jews and Blacks, pernicious as they were, eventually petered out. Then there's Joe McCarthy. He may have been onto something about the communists, but he ruined lots of peoples' lives for 48-point type.

In Circle 6, reserved for heretics, we have Madeline Murray O'Hare eating her words. You see, it's not what went *into* her mouth that doomed her, it's what came *out*. What came out was "God doesn't exist."

Look, even *I* know God exists. Why, just a few weeks ago He called down and said He was sending me Pope Pius XII. He said it was a big mistake the pope got sent to Him, that rerouting him to me had something to do with his caving in to the Nazis. He'll have plenty of company. We have seven other popes down here, but I guess you know that.

Circle 7 is where things get really interesting. Here we have the murderers swimming in blood. God knows there's been no shortage of them in this century. We take them all—the small-timers like John Wayne Gacy and Richard Speck and the big-timers like Joseph Stalin and Pol Pot. Then there's Adolf Hitler, but I'll get to him in a minute.

Circle 8 contains the seducers, flatterers, liars and hypocrites. What's interesting about this group is not who's in but who's on the waiting list—Monica Lewinsky, Bill Clinton, Jimmy Swaggart, Congressman Dan Burton, just to name a few. Off the record, I think Circles 7 and 8 should be switched around, but I'm looking for someone to input my report. It's tough finding good help down here.

In Circle 9 (we're now down to the pit of Hell) we have the traitors—people like Judas Iscariot, frozen in ice for all eternity. Poor chap. I always thought he got a bum rap. At least he showed remorse and hanged himself.

Which is more than I can say for his fellow stiff, Hitler (at least the remorse part). In his last testament, hours before he killed himself, he ranted about how much he hated the Jews and how he was going to settle his score with the German people. He wanted them to be sacked, destroyed, reduced to misery and shame for having failed him.

Call it a technicality, but it was Hitler the traitor, not Hitler the murderer, that wound up in the pit of Hell—kind of like Al Capone's tax evasion rap that landed him in Alcatraz. But in the end he got what he deserved.

I could mention other tyrants from this century, but they're petty by comparison—Slobodan Milosevic, Saddam Hussein, Augusto Pinochet, Idi Amin. Besides, most of them are still on the waiting list. All in all, though, I'm proud of my accomplishments.

Two of my proteges, Hitler and Stalin, are even on *Time* magazine's short list for Person of the Century. I'm really the one whose picture should be on the cover, but nobody knows what I look like. Some artist from Florence, your hometown, got the horns and tail idea from your poem, but the fact is I change my appearance at will. Right now I look like Osama bin Laden.

Yours truly,
Satan

This op-ed piece first appeared in the *Holland* (Michigan) *Sentinel,* December 19, 1999, and was distributed by Tribune Media Services.

Chicago

Oprah, Meet Moses

AUTHOR'S NOTE: This interview is a parody of Oprah Winfrey's infamous interview with James Frey, author of the best-seller A Million Little Pieces, *in which she challenged the truth of Frey's drug addiction story. The interview aired live January 26, 2006, on the "Oprah Winfrey Show" in her Chicago studio. The questions she asks Moses are more or less the same as those she asked Frey. To see the Frey interview online, Google "Frey Winfrey interview."*

OPRAH: On my show today we have one of the patriarchs of the Old Testament, the man who led the Israelites through the wilderness for 40 years, who never got to the Promised Land himself but who saw that his people did, and who claims to have performed several miracles along the way. Let's welcome, please, Moses. (Applause)

MOSES: It's a thrill for me to be on your program. I can't tell you how much I appreciate—

OPRAH: Never mind that. Let's cut to the quick. Is it really true that you wrote the first five books of the Bible, what scholars call the Pentateuch?

MOSES: Yeah, I mean no one else has disputed the claim, so why not go along? Somebody had to write it. It might as well be me.

OPRAH: Let's assume you wrote it then. Lots of questions have come up about its veracity, especially the stories you tell in Genesis.

MOSES: Like what?

OPRAH: Like the story of creation. Are you really saying God created the world in six days?

MOSES: Yeah, I mean like they were very long days, very long days, like billions of years.

OPRAH: Then why didn't you say that? And the story about Adam and Eve, the first two people in the world. Really now, how could two people just pop up at the same time?

No, that isn't Moses with Oprah. It's James Frey defending his book *A Million Little Pieces* against her lie accusations.

MOSES: They were symbolic. I mean they weren't real people.

OPRAH: So you lied.

MOSES (rubbing his nose): I don't remember if they were real people or not.

OPRAH: Come on, Moses, if they were real, who did their sons marry? Their sisters? When siblings cohabit, don't you know what happens to their kids?

MOSES (bewildered): I didn't think of that.

OPRAH: Let's jump ahead to Exodus. There are two episodes in particular I want to ask you about. One is where you write about coming to the Red Sea. The pharoah's army is on your tail and you're looking for an escape route. You wave your staff, and—presto—the Red Sea parts, and you and all your people prance right on through. And when the pharoah's army follows you into the Red Sea, it closes up again and they all drown.

MOSES (rubbing his nose again): Well, I struggled with the idea of it.

OPRAH: No, the lie of it. That's a lie. It's not an idea, Moses. That's a lie.

MOSES (meekly): Yes.

OPRAH: I feel duped. Same with your story about striking a rock and making water flow out of it.

MOSES: Well, I mean I made that up too.

OPRAH: I have to say it's difficult for me to talk to you because I really feel duped. As I sit here today, I don't know what is truth and I don't know what isn't. All my life I grew up thinking everything in the Bible was true.

MOSES (regaining his composure): There's spiritual truth, and there's literal truth. One transcends the other. I still believe in the essential truth of the Bible, which is spiritual truth.

OPRAH: But you're playing fast and loose with the facts, Moses. I read this book as truth.

MOSES: What is truth?

OPRAH: You tell me. You're the writer.

MOSES: Well, I mean I did alter some facts.

OPRAH: I have been really embarrassed by this. I was really behind this book because so many people seem to have gotten so much out of it. But now I feel you conned us all. Don't you?

MOSES: I don't feel like I conned anybody.

This piece appeared simultaneously in the *Holland* (Michigan) *Sentinel* and *Chicago Tribune*, February 9, 2006.

Washington, D.C.

Heeding Our 'Better Angels'

ON MARCH 4, 1861, when our country stood on the brink of civil war, Abraham Lincoln, the newly elected 16th president, stood at the east front of the U.S. Capitol and addressed the crowd.

"We are not enemies, but friends," he said. "Though passion may have strained, it must not break our bonds of affection. The mystic chords of memory...will yet swell the chorus of the Union, when again touched, as they surely will be, by the better angels of our nature."

Lincoln's first inaugural speech wasn't destined to be recited by generations of schoolchildren like his Gettysburg address, but it did capture the national mood. And it expressed his conviction that Americans would reunite after the cannon smoke cleared.

Today, when we find ourselves at another Great Divide, Jon Meacham, the Pulitzer Prize-winning historian, tells us to heed what Lincoln said and give the "better angels" thing another try.

In his latest book, *The Soul of America: The Battle for Our Better Angels,* he reminds us that times like these have tried men's souls before—times marked by hatred, racism, fear, greed, panic. And each time we've managed to come back,

Abe Lincoln was sworn in for the first time at the east front of the U.S. Capitol (still under construction) on March 4, 1861. Four years of civil war were about to follow.

thanks to our better angels. "A tragic element of history," he writes, "is that every advance must contend with the forces of reaction."

On the plus side, we can look back at the New Deal, the Marshall Plan, the Civil Rights Act of 1964, and Neil Armstrong's walk on the moon, to name a few. On the minus side, we have the Ku Klux Klan, the lynchings, the McCarthy witch hunt of the 1950s, the riots on the 1960s, and a whole lot more.

How then, when we're anxious about the future of the country, when a sitting president tears up treaties, sides with dictators, denies climate change, denounces the free press and declares the power to pardon himself, how can we discover our better angels?

Meacham says to do these five things:

1. Enter the arena. Theodore Roosevelt put it this way: "The first duty of an American citizen…is that he shall work in politics; the second is that he shall do that work in a practical manner; and the third is that he shall do it in accord with the highest principles of honor and justice." In other words, work on behalf of the candidates and causes you believe in. Or run for public office yourself.

2. Resist tribalism. Eleanor Roosevelt advised her generation, "Attend not only the meetings of one's own party but of the opposition. Find out what people are saying, what they are thinking, what they believe…. If we are to cope intelligently with a changing world, we must be flexible and willing to relinquish our opinions." Translated today: Don't let any single cable network or Twitter feed tell you what to think.

3. Respect facts and deploy reason. John Adams said facts are stubborn things. Yet too many Americans are locked into their particular vision of the world, choosing this view or that based not on its grounding in fact but whether it's endorsed by the leaders they follow. "The dictators of the world," Harry Truman wrote, "say if you tell a lie often enough, people will

believe it." Remember that the next time you attend a political rally.

4. Find a critical balance. In 1789, Thomas Jefferson wrote, "Wherever the people are well-informed they can be trusted with their own government." Being informed is more than knowing details and arguments. It entails being humble enough to recognize that only on the rarest of occasions does any single camp have a monopoly on virtue or wisdom.

5. Keep history in mind. Daniel Webster drew this analogy from the sea: "When the mariner has been tossed for many days in thick weather, and on an unknown sea, he avails himself of the first pause in the storm…to take his latitude and ascertain how far the elements have driven him from his true course." In like manner, consider how we fit into the grand scheme of things. History gives us a frame of reference. To remember Joe McCarthy, for instance, helps us to know a demagogue when we see one.

Remember these things the next time you step into a voting booth.

This op-ed piece first appeared in the *Holland Sentinel*, November 2, 2018, and was syndicated by the Tribune News Service.

Philadelphia

Our Republic: Can We Keep It?

AT THE CLOSE OF THE Constitutional Convention in 1787 an elderly woman approached Benjamin Franklin as he was leaving the Pennsylvania State House. "Tell me, Dr. Franklin," she said. "Do we have a republic or a monarchy?"

Dr. Franklin replied, "A republic, madam, if you can keep it."

If our Founding Fathers could come back, what would they think about our country today? Would they turn over in their graves? Or would they be astounded that our republic is still alive?

George Washington, who presided at the 1787 Convention, predicted the new American republic wouldn't last 20 years. So take a guess.

Next to July 4, 1776, when we declared our independence from Great Britain, September 17, 1787, is probably the most important day in American history. That's when our Founding Fathers signed the U.S. Constitution. Yet we pay scant attention to what they accomplished on that date.

The late Chief Justice Earl Warren observed: "Our Constitution was not a grant of power from government to the people...but a grant of power by the people to the government which they—the people—had created." Until

The cartoon got the words right but the date wrong. It was in 1787, after the Constitutional Convention, that Ben Franklin, issued his famous warning.

our Founding Fathers figured this out, monarchies were the rule, and rule they did, by blood—in more ways than one.

In framing our Constitution, our Founders took into account the history of governments and determined a way to prevent injustice and repression that too often characterized them. The result was the fairest and most enduring agreement between government and the governed the world has known.

Yet even our best effort at self-government has its problems. Human nature hasn't changed. Greed, self-interest, corruption and petty hates are inherent in any form of government. Recognizing that, our Founders devised a way in which human error in the operation of government would at least occur in the open. They disdained the best-man theory of government that said, "Put the right people into office and government will take care of itself." History was littered with the wreckage of governments headed by good men gone wrong.

So where are we heading?

That depends. If, because of apathy or our dislike of candidates, we don't vote, we put our republic at risk. In the 2016 presidential election, 43 percent of eligible voters—about 100 million U.S. citizens—didn't vote. That's not good. To abandon the ballot box is to abandon our right and obligation as American citizens.

In spite of Washington's prediction, our republic is now the oldest in the world; our constitution is the most enduring and the model for democracies around the globe. That isn't to say our constitution is perfect. It didn't produce heaven on earth or solve all our problems. But it did provide a framework for working out our own version of life, liberty, and the pursuit of happiness.

And the day our Founders accomplished that is a day worth celebrating.

This op-ed piece first appeared in the *Holland* (Michigan) *Sentinel*, September 17, 2019, and was syndicated by the Tribune News Service.

Bedford Falls

Just How Bad Was 2020?

IF YOUR HOUSEHOLD is like mine, the Frank Capra movie "It's a Wonderful Life" is as much a holiday staple as Charles Dickens' "A Christmas Carol."

James Stewart plays George Baily, a well-meaning, small-town mortgage lender who helps people buy their homes instead of having to rent them from a slumlord. But he's discouraged by how his life is going. It gets so bad he even contemplates suicide.

On Christmas Eve, his guardian angel spares him that fate and shows him what his hometown would be like had he never been born. Brought back to reality, George finds that his life isn't so bad after all. In fact, his life is, well, quite wonderful.

It all has to do with perspective.

The same can be said for 2020. Last week *Time* magazine pronounced it "The Worst Year Ever." Not since the spread of fascism in the 1930s, wrote Stephanie Zacharek in her cover story, "have we been faced with so many abnormal events that have been so egregiously distorted by aberrant leadership."

I hate to say it, but she's right. In 2020, we witnessed apocalyptic wildfires in the West, devastating hurricanes in the South, the murders of George Floyd and Breonna Taylor by Minneapolis and Louisville police, our democracy reduced to life support thanks to a president who tried every trick up his sleeve to kill it.

When Frank Capra's "It's a Wonderful Life" came out in 1946, it was a box office flop.
Since then it has become a holiday classic.

Even worse, we suffered through a preventable pandemic that killed more than 300,000 people—five times the death rate of the rest of the world—and destroyed millions of livelihoods.

Make no mistake, 2020 was a pretty bad year. But when you compare it to other bad years from our past, maybe it wasn't as bad as you think.

Take 1919, for example, when the Spanish flu took more than 50 million lives worldwide, and this after World War I killed 20 million and devastated Europe.

Or 1968 when Martin Luther King Jr. and Bobby Kennedy were assassinated, when dozens of American cities were set on fire, when the Vietnam War split our country apart, when a million lives were lost to the Hong Kong flu.

Or any year of the Civil War.

In the broad scheme of things, maybe 2020 wasn't so bad after all. Writer Daniel Riley, in *GQ* magazine, ventured there might even be an upside. "For so many aspects of life that needed changing, the pandemic was an accelerant."

How can that be?

As bad as it was, 2020 showed us new ways of doing things. It showed us the benefits of working at home. It showed us how to reduce carbon emissions by driving and flying less. It showed us how to reimagine our cities with outdoor restaurants and streets closed to traffic.

Above all, it showed us how to value what matters in life. More Scrabble games, more Monopoly, more conversations with family and friends—even if we have to do them on Zoom.

Let's hope we'll look back on 2020 someday—as George Bailey might have—not as a year of disaster, but as a year of rebirth.

This op-ed piece first appeared in the *Holland* (Michigan) *Sentinel*, December 28, 2020, and was syndicated by the Tribune News Service.

Acknowledgments

I owe a huge debt of gratitude to the many editors I have worked with through the years, first and foremost the late Randy VandeWater, my mentor and editor at the *Holland* (Michigan) *Sentinel* in the town where I grew up. Others are Neal Shine of the *Detroit Free Press;* my colleagues at Wayne State University—Paul Pentecost, Mike Sibille and Bill White (it was Bill's book *By-Line: Ernest Hemingway* that inspired this one); Pat Colburn and Paul Povse of the Springfield, Illinois, *State Journal-Register,* and the succession of editors and staff writers at the *Chicago Tribune* with whom I worked for nearly four nearly decades—Jack Fuller, Jeff Lyon, Pete Gorner, Bob Goldsborough, Elizabeth Taylor, Al Borcover, Charles Madigan and Tom Stites, the *Tribune*'s Tempo editor in the 1980s with whom I've had the joy to reconnect in the past year. In defiance of Thomas Wolfe's assertion that you can't go home again, I returned to Holland, my home town, a quarter century ago. Since then I've had the pleasure of working with three of Randy's successors at the *Sentinel*: Jim Timmermann, Ben Beversluis and Sarah Leach. The op-ed pieces in Part Three are representative of those years. To my friends who continue to labor in the vineyards of print journalism, I say keep up the good work. Our democracy depends on it.

Photo & Illustration Credits

Page:

6 Student with Israeli flag. Photo taken at Auschwitz-Birkenau, 2016. (Reuters)

14 Milton Nieuwsma photo by Fred Henry, 1986. (*Chicago Tribune*)

21 Yagua native photo by Milton Nieuwsma, 1987. (*Los Angeles Times*)

30 Nubian desert dweller photo by Milton Nieuwsma, 1989. (*New York Daily News*)

38 *Endurance* photo by Frank Hurley, 1915. (*Associated Press*)

45 Noah's ark painting by Simon de Myle, 1570. (Public domain)

53 Terracotta soldiers photo by Milton Nieuwsma, 2013. (*Chicago Tribune*)

57 Kizhi Island photo by M. Plaskin, 2014. (*Orthodox Christianity*)

62 Mont-Saint-Michel photo by Milton Nieuwsma, 1985. (*State Journal- Register*)

66 Field of Dreams photos. Top: by Milton Nieuwsma, 1990. (*Los Angeles Times*) Bottom: file photo, August 21, 2021. (*Des Moines Register*)

71 Woodcut of Virginia Dare christening, August 24, 1587. Artist unknown. (Bettmann Archives)

81 Jefferson portrait by Mather Brown, 1786. (National Portrait Gallery)

93 Presidential Medal of Freedom presentation, January 10, 1977. (White House Archives)

102 Emmett Till photo by Mamie Till-Mobley, December 25, 1954. (*Chicago Tribune*)

113 Kinderlager photo by Soviet army photographer, January 27-28, 1945. (Public domain)

120 Pete VandenBosch, c. 2010. (*Holland Sentinel*)

131 Detail of "The Last Judgment" by Michelangelo, 1568. (Sistine Chapel)

136 James Frey and Oprah Winfrey, January 26, 2006. (Harpo Productions)

140 Lincoln's first inauguration, March 4, 1861. Photographer unknown. (Public domain)

144 Detail of cartoon by Etta Hulme, March 6, 1999. (*Fort Worth Star-Telegram*)

147 Poster by RKO Radio Pictures, 1946. (Public domain)

About the Author

Milton Nieuwsma, a two-time Emmy Award winning writer and journalist, traveled around the world for many years covering stories for the *Chicago Tribune* and other major newspapers. He is the writer and creator of the acclaimed PBS series *Inventing America* and the author or co-author of seven books including *Kinderlager*, named "Best Book for Teens" by the New York Public Library. In 2009 Hope College honored him with a Distinguished Alumni Award. Milt and his wife Marilee have three children and seven grandchildren and live in Holland, Michigan.

For sales, editorial information, subsidiary rights information
or a catalog, please write or phone or e-mail
AbsolutelyAmazingEbooks
Manhanset House
Shelter Island Hts., New York 11965-0342, US
Tel: 212-427-7139
www.BrickTowerPress.com
bricktower@aol.com
www.IngramContent.com

For sales in the UK and Europe please contact our distributor,
Gazelle Book Services
White Cross Mills
Lancaster, LA1 4XS, UK
Tel: (01524) 68765 Fax: (01524) 63232
email: jacky@gazellebooks.co.uk

www.ingramcontent.com/pod-product-compliance
Lightning Source LLC
Chambersburg PA
CBHW060623310726
48982CB00003B/654

* 9 7 8 1 8 7 6 9 6 9 0 9 7 *